WHO WAS A JEW?

Rabbinic and Halakhic Perspectives
on the Jewish Christian Schism

WHO WAS A JEW?

Rabbinic and Halakhic Perspectives
on the Jewish Christian Schism

by

LAWRENCE H. SCHIFFMAN

KTAV PUBLISHING HOUSE
BROOKLYN, NEW YORK
2019

Published by
KTAV PUBLISHING HOUSE
527 Empire Blvd.
Brooklyn, NY 11225
orders@ktav.com | www.ktav.com
(718) 972-5449

ISBN 978-0-88125-054-1

Library of Congress Cataloging in Publication Data

Schiffman, Lawrence H.
    Who was a Jew?

    Bibliography: p.
    Includes index.
    1. Tannaim.   2. Jews—Identity.   3. Proselytes and
proselyting, Jewish.   4. Judaism—Relations—Christianity.
5. Christianity and other religions—Judaism.   I. Title.
BM501.2.S3   1985   296.3'872   84-17144
ISBN 0-88125-053-8
ISBN 0-88125-054-6 (pbk.)

Manufactured in the United States of America

To our children

דניאל אברהם נ״י
הדסה בתיה שתחי׳
לאה דבורה שתחי׳
אסתר טובה שתחי׳

הבנים עטרה לאבות (בראשית רבא סג:ב)

Contents

VII. Conclusion: The Final Break 75

Preface

In recent years the issue of "Who is a Jew?" has become predominant in the Jewish community, both in America and Israel. The debate has generated a considerable literature and has involved some of the foremost scholars in the field of Judaica. Yet the fact that this same issue was of paramount importance previously in Jewish history has somehow escaped attention. The halakhic questions of Jewish status and identity were, as we shall see, the overriding reason that Rabbinic Judaism sometime in the second century C.E. ceased to regard the Christians as a sect of Jews and began to regard them as another people.

My own interest in this subject was aroused when Professor E. P. Sanders of McMaster University in Hamilton, Ontario, invited me to participate in a symposium on the subject of "Normative Self-Definition in Judaism from the Maccabees to the Mid-Third Century," held at McMaster in June 1979. The symposium was part of a continuing research project at McMaster University on Jewish and Christian self-definition, funded by a grant from the Social Sciences and Humanities Research Council of Canada. The papers presented at the symposium were published in *Jewish and Christian Self-Definition*, Volume II, *Aspects of Judaism in the Greco-Roman Period*, edited by E. P. Sanders, with A. I. Baumgarten and A. Mendelson (London: SCM Press, Philadelphia: Fortress Press, 1981).

The purpose of the McMaster project was to probe "the process of achieving normative self-definition," in Judaism and Christianity, meaning the process whereby the two religions narrowed the options of what it meant to be Jewish or Christian, excluded other options, and took measures to assure that favored positions would become normative. The questions raised by the McMaster symposium led to my contribution, "At the Crossroads: Tannaitic Perspectives on the Jewish Christian Schism," and also raised for me many fundamental questions about the history of Judaism in Late Antiquity.

It was therefore with enthusiasm that I took up the suggestion of my good friend Mr. Bernard Scharfstein of Ktav Publishing House, Inc., that I expand the original paper into a book. In so doing I hope to have widened the context of the original study somewhat and to have added material originally omitted for reasons of space. At the same time, the questions addressed are essentially those posed by the McMaster symposium, and I am extremely grateful to Professor E. P. Sanders not only for his invitation, but also for the many suggestions he made regarding the original manuscript. Professor David Halivni of the Jewish Theological Seminary of America, also a participant in the symposium, made careful comments on the Rabbinic material, and I am most appreciative of his help. Dr. Daniel J. Lasker of Ben Gurion University of the Negev, himself an authority on Jewish-Christian relations in the medieval period, was kind enough to review the original paper as well. Professor Stuart Miller of the University of Connecticut undertook to read the completed manuscript of this study. As always, I am indebted to my colleagues at the Department of Near Eastern Languages and Literatures and the Hagop Kevorkian Center for Near Eastern Studies of New York University, especially Professor Francis E. Peters, Chairman of the Department, and Professor Baruch A. Levine for their encouragement and for the opportunity to discuss aspects of this work with them. This volume would have been impossible without the kindness of Professor Sanders and Miss M. Lydamore, Associate Editor of SCM Press Ltd. of London, who graciously granted me permission to reuse that material which had originally appeared in the McMaster volume. My wife, Marlene, undertook the typing and preparation of the manuscript as well as that of the Glossary, Bibliography and Index. The volume is dedicated to our children, who, in the words of the Midrash (*Bereshit Rabbah* 63:2), are a crown to their parents.

List of Abbreviations

For short title references or fuller bibliographic description, see the Bibliography.

Ant.	Josephus, *Antiquities of the Jews*
B.	*Babylonian Talmud*
ed. princ.	*editio princeps* (first printed edition)
ed. Krot.	*Palestinian Talmud*, Krotoschin edition
EJ	*Encyclopaedia Judaica*
H.	*Hilkhot* in M. Maimonides, *Mishneh Torah*
Hom.	*Homilies*
HUCA	*Hebrew Union College Annual*
ILR	*Israel Law Review*
JBL	*Journal of Biblical Literature*
JE	*The Jewish Encyclopedia*
JJS	*Journal of Jewish Studies*
JQR	(o.s., n.s.), *Jewish Quarterly Review* (original series, new series)
KS	*Kiryat Sepher*
M.	Mishnah
P.	*Palestinian Talmud*
PG	Jacques Paul Migne, *Patrologiae Cursus Completus . . . Series Graeca* (Paris, 1844–65)
T.	Tosefta
TK	S. Lieberman, *Tosefta' Ki-Fshutah*
TR	S. Lieberman, *Tosefet Rishonim*
Vat. Ebr.	Vatican Hebrew Manuscript
ZHB	*Zeitschrift für Hebraische Bibliographie*

I. Introduction: At the Crossroads

During the entire length of the Second Temple period, Judaism had tolerated sectarianism and schism.[1] Yet by the end of the tannaitic period, Christianity was to be regarded as another religion entirely. This study will concentrate on the attitude of Judaism in the pre-Christian and early Christian periods to Jewish identity and the nascent Christian Church. It will seek to understand why Christianity was not simply regarded as one of the sects, and why, when, and how Judaism sought to dissociate itself fully from Christianity.

The Second Temple period was crucial for the emergence of the Jews and Judaism from the land-based, Near Eastern concept of peoplehood, of which we read in the Bible, to the self-image of a world religion. To be sure, the ancient Israelites already believed that their God was God over the entire world and that He controlled the heavenly bodies as well. But this theology was never acted out as long as Israel remained in its ancestral homeland, except insofar as the Israelites welcomed those who sought to join them.

Yet at the start of the Second Temple period the issues of Jewish identity came to the fore immediately when questions of intermarriage and the legitimacy of the Samaritans as "Jews" had to be discussed in our sources.[2] Clearly these events reflected a transitional period between the extended tribes of Israel and the Jewish people, and the attendant view of Judaism as a world religion was only beginning to become a reality. This can be seen in the groping of the small Jewish community of mercenaries at Elephantine in the Persian period, who still did not know how to practice Judaism outside the Land of Israel. We can imagine that the Jews of the Babylonian exile suffered such confusion throughout the Persian period. This confusion only abated when Judaism adjusted to its status as a world religion in the Hellenistic period.

The Second Temple period in Jewish history can be defined in hindsight as a period of struggle between various competing ideologies for the future of Judaism. It began with the exclusion of the Samaritans from the Jewish people and ended with the final schism which left Judaism and Christianity as separate religions. Yet throughout this period numerous sects and groups populated the Jewish world, each with its own ideology and interpretation of the Torah.

In the early years of the Hellenistic period, the Jewish people became further acquainted with Hellenism. Their earlier contacts had been largely commercial. The new era which had dawned placed the Jews under the political domination of the competing Hellenistic empires, the Seleucids and the Ptolemies, and brought in its wake the inevitable cultural and even religious influences. Indeed, these new circumstances simply plunged the Jewish people right back into the old problems of the prophetic age, with the encroachment of pagan practices and influences. And so the first issue to be addressed was the degree of acceptance of the Hellenistic way of life.[3]

Extreme Hellenizers favored allowing Judaism to become one of the Hellenistic cults. Under these circumstances the Jews would be able to share in the cultural and all-important economic opportunities of the Hellenistic world. But the masses of the Jewish people under Hasmonean leadership indicated their unwillingness to accept so extreme a compromise with the new world order. Instead, the people favored a less radical modus vivendi.

Even here competing approaches grew up. Some, like the priestly and aristocratic classes later to become the Sadducees, favored a greater openness to the new environment. Others, like the Pharisees and the common people (whom the Rabbis later called the 'am ha-'areṣ) favored greater separation from the new influences and adherence to the old Near Eastern way of life.

Still other issues divided the people. In the aftermath of the Hasmonean revolt, various ideologies emerged, as manifested in the Pharisees, Sadducees, Essenes, and Dead Sea sect and a host of other groups, some apocalyptic and Messianic, which competed for the hearts of the people. Messianic fervor was manifested in the many apocalyptic sects as well as in the constant agitation for revolt. This fervor eventually swept the Jewish people into the Great Revolt of 66–74 C.E.

Although the Pharisees, Sadducees, Essenes, Dead Sea sect, and others disagreed on fundamental issues of theology, law, biblical exegesis, and social and political matters, no sect ever claimed that the others were not Jews. Rather, all groups implicitly recognized the Jewish status of their competitors. Even in regard to the extreme Hellenists, the claim was never made that they had somehow left the Jewish people by their apostasy.

As the Second Commonwealth period was drawing to a close, the Great Revolt was to bring an end to this wide variety of groups. The Sadducees were unable to survive the war as a viable group since the Temple which had been their power base was destroyed, and the Roman powers turned away from the Sadducees as political leaders for the Jewish people. The Dead Sea sect, and probably other similar groups, were decimated by the Roman troops. The extreme Messianism of other apocalyptics led them to participation in the revolt, and the bulk of these were likewise decimated. Only two groups were to survive the revolt.

The Pharisees had long shown an adaptability which would serve them well in the post-destruction era. They would adapt to the new political realities and emerge as the internal rulers of the Jewish people of Palestine. From a religious point of view, the destruction would end a long process through which Pharisaic Judaism was becoming increasingly centered on home and synagogue and less reliant on Temple and cult. This meant that in post-Temple times the Pharisees, later called tannaim, would present a formula for the survival of the Jewish people and their ancestral religion which would carry the day.

Yet in the last days of the Second Temple, the beginning of a schism was taking place in the Jewish people. Some Jews, fanned by two hundred years of Messianic speculation, centered in such groups as the sect of Qumran and those who produced the apocalyptic writings preserved in the Apocrypha and pseudepigrapha, were to come to believe in the Messiahship of one Jesus of Nazareth.

Rather than concern ourselves with the historical circumstances of the ministry of Jesus and the rise of Christianity, we will focus on a unique element in the history of this particular Jewish sect. Whereas all the other Jewish sects and ideologies of the Second Commonwealth remained within the Jewish fold regardless of how radical they may have been, this one group eventually diverged and became a separate "religion." Our study will seek to determine why and how this happened. The research presented here will be based largely on tannaitic evidence for two reasons. First, by the time Judaism and Christianity made their final break, it was the tannaitic tradition which was almost completely representative of the Jewish community in Palestine and, to a great extent, of that segment of the Diaspora which remained loyal to its ancestral faith. Second, the evidence available does not indicate any difference of opinion regarding Jewish status between the various sects of the Second Commonwealth and later tannaitic traditions.[4]

It can be argued that it is purely by coincidence that disagreements regarding the subject of Jewish identity did not come down to us. However, it is most likely that there were none. Indeed, contention regarding the very notions of who was a Jew and who a Gentile would have been of such great importance as to figure prominently in the sources. Further, nothing could have served as a more forceful polemic than to accuse opposing sects of not being Jewish. Yet despite all the sectarian animus found in various texts from or about the Second Commonwealth period,[5] even the most virulent never accuse the members of other groups of having left the Jewish community. Sinners they were, but Jews all the same.

What then caused the Jews of the tannaitic period to reject the Christians? Let us examine how the Jews viewed their own identity and how they evaluated Christianity and the Christians within this framework. (Beyond our concern will be the attitude of the Christians to Judaism and the self-definition of the early Christian communities.)

The causes of the Jewish-Christian schism may be classified in two categories—doctrinal and socio-historical. In Judaism the doctrinal factors are expressed through the *halakhah,* the Jewish legal system. Indeed, it is the *halakhah* which may be described as that which typifies Rabbinic Judaism. One who seeks to understand Rabbinic Judaism must base his investigation on its legal teachings, for they were formative in the history of Judaism.[6] In order to grasp the distinction between Jew and Christian as understood from the tannaitic point of view, it will be necessary to inquire into the definitions of the Jew at this time. We shall have to know what constituted an indigenous member of the Jewish people, a born Jew, and what requirements existed for conversion. Only in this way will we be able to understand how the Rabbis treated the early Christians and how they reacted to the shift from Jewish to Gentile Christianity. We shall also have to investigate the tannaitic views of heresy as applied to the early Christians and to determine the impact of these laws. The traditions to be examined must also be dated as precisely as possible to be certain that they do, in fact, form part of the background for the parting of Judaism and Christianity.

The socio-historical factors are the result of the evolution of Judaism and Christianity in this period. Specifically, the Jewish attitude towards Christianity was influenced greatly by the changes that took place in the emerging Church during the first two centuries of this era. Only by considering these changes will it be possible to understand why the Jewish self-definition led the Rabbis to regard Christians first as heretics and later as members of a separate and distinct religious community.

It is in the nature of all societies and groups that certain formal

or informal regulations exist regarding membership in the group
and the behavior of the members. Religious groups, in addition to
adherence to their codes of behavior and belief, also mandate
requirements for membership or rites of initiation. These procedures may differ depending on whether the member stands in
hereditary relationship to other members or whether he is an entirely new member, usually termed a convert. The requirements for
membership or entry into religious groups would have no significance if they were but arbitrary or accidental. However, we know
them to reflect the perceptions of the group about its own identity
and nature. We can, therefore, learn a great deal about a religious
group from the study of its regulations for membership or conversion. We can understand how the group characterizes itself and its
relationship to the society within which it functions. Conversely, we
can compare the perceptions of the society at large with the group's
requirements and regulations. Is the group's image of itself consis-
tent with that of outsiders or not, and what do outsiders consider
the basic character of the religious group?

Within this framework this study will seek to determine what the
requirements were for hereditary membership in the tannaitic
Jewish community, and how one could enter the Jewish people as a
convert. From these regulations we will see what the Rabbis regarded as the essence of Judaism and Jewish identity. The history of the
legal practices we encounter will be examined to see how far back
the tannaitic approach can be traced.

Most important is the establishment of the halakhic definitions
of a Jew which existed in the period in which Christianity developed.
After we consider how one may enter the Jewish people, we will ask
whether it is possible to leave or to be expelled from the polity of
Israel. We shall see that a Jew continued to be regarded as a Jew by
the tannaim even if he espoused Christianity. However, the tannaim
did impose legal sanctions upon the early Jewish Christians whom
they regarded as transgressors, but Jews nonetheless. Eventually, as
the Christians turned further and further away from the halakhic

definitions of a Jew, the tannaitic sources portray a progressive exclusion of the Christians. Once Christianity became almost completely Gentile, from the halakhic point of view, the final break took place. It is, therefore, the *halakhah* regarding who was a Jew which, to the tannaim, ultimately determined the expulsion of the Christians from the Jewish community and the establishment of Christianity as a separate "religion."[7]

II. The Jew by Birth

Before documenting the response of the tannaim to the rise of Christianity, we shall have to discuss at length the definitions of a Jew which were in effect at the time of the Jewish-Christian schism. After all, the attitude of the early Rabbis to the emerging Christian group, we shall see, was to a large part determined by this question. The tannaim would assess the early Christians, specifically their status as Jews or Gentiles, from the perspective of the *halakhah*. We shall have to establish the definitions of both the born Jew and the proselyte. In doing so, we will pay close attention to problems of dating so as to be certain that the *halakhot* we are studying would have been in force by the time of the Jewish-Christian schism.

The Tannaitic Definition

The starting point for the understanding of the tannaitic definition of the Jew must be M. Qiddushin 3:12 and the complementary T. Qiddushin 4:16. M. Qiddushin 3:12 states:[1]

> (If) any (woman) is disqualified from marrying not only[2] this (man) but also any other (Jew), (then her) child is equal in status to her. And to what (case) does this (refer)? This (refers to) the child of a bond-woman[3] or a non-Jewess.[4]

9

Here the Mishnah is discussing the question of the personal status of the offspring of various unions. It first deals with the offspring of a legitimate marriage in which the status of the child (priest, Levite, Israelite) is determined by the lineage of the father. It then discusses cases in which the marriage involves a transgression of marriage law but in which the marriage is nonetheless considered valid. These are cases in which a person married someone of lower status, and the law fixes the status of the child as that of the inferior partner (whether the mother or the father). Then the Mishnah discusses the *mamzer,* the offspring of a prohibited marriage[5] in which the woman would have been permitted (by virtue of her Jewish status) to marry another man. Finally, the Mishnah comes to the case quoted above and indicates that in a marriage between a Jewish man and a bondwoman or non-Jewess, the status of the child is the same as that of the mother.

Can this text be dated? J. N. Epstein[6] has noted that M. Qiddushin 3:12–4:14 constitutes a literary unit to which he refers as a "tractate of forbidden marriages and pedigrees."[7] He sees the anonymous material, constituting almost the entire text, as coming from the period before the destruction of the Temple. While there is no way of confirming Epstein's dating, it is certain that the named material in this section has been interpolated into a previously existing "text." In view of the identity of the named authorities, all of whom flourished in the Yavnean period, we should have to say that our mishnah would date, if not from the time the Temple stood, then at the latest from the Yavnean period. We can therefore set a *terminus ad quem* for the mishnah of 125 C.E. It should be noted that this ruling is not contested in any tannaitic sources.[8]

What if a child were born to a Jewish woman and a non-Jewish man? T. Qiddushin 4:16 supplies the answer:[9]

> If a non-Jew or a slave had intercourse[10] with a Jewish woman, and she gave birth[11] to a child, the offspring is a *mamzer.* Rabbi Simeon ben Judah[12] says in the name of Rabbi Simeon:[13] The child is not a *mamzer* unless it is (the offspring of a Jewish man) from a woman who

is forbidden to him by the laws of prohibited consanguineous marriages ('*erwah*)[14] and on account of (having intercourse with) whom he is liable to the punishment of excision (*karet*).[15]

This passage presents a debate as to whether a child born from the union of a non-Jew or slave and a Jewish woman is considered a *mamzer* or not.[16] We can loosely translate *mamzer* as one whose ancestry disqualified him from marriage with free, hereditary Jews of the priestly, Levitical, or Israelite classes.[17] The often-used translation "bastard" or "illegitimate offspring" is misleading, since it conjures up the western legal systems in which one born out of wedlock is so stigmatized. Here we refer to one born of a union which is itself illegal. There is, however, some controversy as to whether all forbidden unions confer the status of *mamzerut* or only some. The anonymous teacher of the first part of our tosefta statement believes that the offspring of a Jewish mother and non-Jewish father is a *mamzer*,[18] while Rabbi Simeon disagrees.[19]

To grasp the full significance of this dispute for our study, we must remember that *mamzerim* are considered full-fledged Jews from all points of view except that of marriage law. They are obligated to observe the commandments and may bear witness. In short, they are Jews, albeit of low estate.[20] It is generally assumed that the stigmatization of the offspring of illegal marriage was intended to serve as a deterrent to such unions. On the other hand, the laws of *mamzerut* may be the result of the tendency of all societies to look down upon children whose parents' union represented a violation of the norms of the society, which, in turn, was viewed as an infringement upon the cosmic order.

Our dispute, then, makes it clear that the offspring of the union of a Jewish woman and a non-Jewish man was certainly considered a Jew. Can we arrive at any dating of the tosefta passage? Here again we are dealing with a unit of anonymous statements into which occasional named glosses representing variant views have been interpolated. R. Simeon ben Judah is a fourth-generation tanna, and it might have been expected that the tradition he handed down was that of Simeon ben Yoḥai, a third-generation tanna who lived during and after the Bar Kokhba rebellion. On the other hand, M. Yevamot 4:13 cites a similar view in the name of Simeon the Temanite. It seems, then, that he is the Simeon of our tosefta. The anonymous view expressed in the first clause of our tosefta passage is most probably identical to that of Rabbi Akiva in M. Yevamot 4:13[21] and assumed by M. Yevamot 7:5.[22]

M. Yevamot 4:13 fixes the law according to Simeon the Temanite who lived in the period of the Yavneh Sanhedrin (80–125 C.E.). By his time there was certainly no question of the Jewishness of the offspring of a Jewish mother and a non-Jewish father, while the child of a non-Jewish mother and a Jewish father was not considered to be a Jew.[23] How early can these rulings be documented?

Josephus assumes this requirement to have been in effect in the early Herodian period. In Ant. XIV, xv, 2 (399–405) Josephus tells us that when Herod surrounded Jerusalem in 39 B.C.E. with the help of the Roman general Silo, Herod instructed his men to make a proclamation to the inhabitants of the city of his willingness to grant amnesty to those who had resisted him in the past. Antigonus responded that (para. 403):[24]

> It would be contrary to their own notion of right if they gave the kingship to Herod who was a commoner and an Idumaean, that is, a half-Jew, when they ought to offer it to those who were of the race, as was their custom.

Scholars have taken the Greek γένος, translated here as "race,"[25] to refer to the royal family.[26] But we know that Herod's father, Antipater, was a descendant of those Idumeans forcibly converted to Judaism by John Hyrcanus.[27] Herod's mother, however, was Cypros of a Nabatean noble family,[28] and no claim of her conversion to Judaism is made in our sources, even in those favorable to Herod. Hence, the narrative terms him a half-Jew, meaning one not legitimately Jewish because his mother was not Jewish. The text of Josephus then indicates that according to what the Rabbis later

called *halakhah* (for which Greek ἔθος, "custom," is the technical
term in Josephus[29]), it was not permitted for one legally a non-Jew
to serve as king over the Jewish nation.[30]

It is uncertain, however, whether this exchange between the last
of the Hasmonean kings and Herod is to be accepted as historical. It
is not found in the parallel in War I, xv, 5 (295–6), where only the
proclamation and counter-exhortations are mentioned. It can be
that some pro-Hasmonean source later added this claim on behalf
of the superior right of the Hasmoneans to kingship and the illegitimacy of Herod as ruler over the Jews. Nonetheless, this claim could
credibly be attributed to Antigonus, since we shall see that the ruling
in question was already in effect in early Second Temple times. While
we are left in a quandary about the exact historical facts, the validity
of such an argument and the possibility that it might have been
made by Antigonus are within reason. To be sure, the passage shows
that by Josephus' time, the regulations in question were normative
in the Palestinian Jewish community.

The fact that Herod's mother was not Jewish is likewise reflected
in M. Sotah 7:8:[31]

> Agrippa the King stood, took (the Torah scroll) and read (it) stand-
> ing,[32] and the Sages praised him. And when he came (to),[33] "You
> must not set a foreigner over you (as king) who is not your brother,"
> (Deut. 17:15) his tears welled up.[34] They (the Sages) said to him, "Do
> not fear Agrippa. You are our brother! You are our brother!"

Agrippa knew of his ancestry on his father's side and was aware
that to the Pharisaic sages of his time Herod's status had been that
of a non-Jew. For this reason he cried when he reached the Torah's
requirement that only a full-fledged Jew serve as king. The Sages
reassured him by saying that he was indeed a Jew, as his ancestry on
his mother's side was Jewish.

There has been extensive debate as to whether the Agrippa of
our Mishnaic text is Agrippa I (10 B.C.E.–44 C.E.) or Agrippa II (28
C.E.–92 C.E.).[35] Agrippa I was a grandson of Herod and Mariamne,

the Hasmonean princess. Their son, Aristobulus, married Berenice, daughter of the Idumaean Costobar and Herod's sister, Salome. Salome was certainly not of Jewish ancestry on her mother's side. Costobar actually opposed the Judaizing of the Idumaeans.[36] Clearly, then, the Sages could not have responded, "You are our brother!" to Agrippa I, since his mother, Berenice, was not of Jewish descent according to the *halakhah*. On the other hand, Agrippa II was a son of Agrippa I. His mother was Cypros II, daughter of Herod's brother, Phasael, and Salampsio. Now Salampsio was the daughter of Herod and of Mariamne, the Hasmonean princess. This means that Agrippa II was fully Jewish according to the legal definition, and it can only be to him that the Mishnah would have pictured the Sages as having replied: "You are our brother!"[37]

The Biblical Background

Several biblical passages prohibit the marriage of Israelites with the previous inhabitants of the land of Canaan. Ex. 34:15 indicates that covenants with the inhabitants of the land (*yoshev ha-'ares*) are forbidden lest they lead to participation in pagan worship and, as a result, to the marriage of pagans to Israelite girls. Deut. 7:1–4 specifically refers to the Hittites, Girgashites, Amorites, Canaanites, Perizzites, Hivites, and Jebusites, the seven nations who are elsewhere said to have been the original inhabitants of the land. After commanding the utter destruction of these nations, the passage again repeats the prohibition of entering into a covenant with them and specifies that intermarriage with them, either on the male or female side, is prohibited. For intermarriage will result in the turning away of the sons,[38] who will worship idols (cf. Josh. 23:7, 12f.).[39]

In addition, Deut. 23:4–7 imposes further restrictions on nations which may not "enter the congregation." These passages as well are usually understood to proscribe intermarriage. The Ammonites and Moabites are prohibited forever, for they refused to supply food and water to Israel after the Exodus and hired Balaam to curse Israel. Deut. 23:8f. indicates that the Egyptians and Edomites may "enter the congregation" according to the Torah only in the third generation. 1 Kings 11:1f. says that inter-marriage was forbidden with Moabite, Ammonite, Edomite, Sidonian, and Hittite women. The editor of Kings simply updated the names of those very same seven nations of pre-Israelite Canaan in accord with the realities of his day.

One of the first problems Ezra faced upon his arrival from Baby-lonia was the existence of mixed marriages (Ezra 9–10). Returning Judean exiles had married non-Israelite women, and children had been born to them. These women were from the '*ame ha-'araṣot*, "the peoples of the land." The suggestion was made by one of the leaders that the people enter into a covenant to expel these wives and their children, the proper procedure according to "the commandment of our God and according to the Torah" (Ezra 10:3). Ezra accepted this suggestion, and the people swore to put it into effect.

Y. Kaufmann[40] is probably correct in assuming that there could not have been an institution for religious conversion at this time. According to him, conversion was originally accomplished by attachment to the land and collective fate of the people of Israel. The early Second Commonwealth, however, was a period of transi-tion. The old process, followed for example by Ruth,[41] had gone out of use, yet the later methods of conversion, based upon a conception of Judaism as a religion rather than Israel as a national entity, had not yet developed.[42] It is only in this light that one can understand why conversion was not employed to avoid the separation of fami-lies and the hardships it must have brought about.

It is not necessary to concern ourselves here with the halakhic *midrash* which served Ezra as the basis of his conclusion that all these marriages were illegal.[43] What must be noted is a peculiar contrast between the narrative material in Ezra and the legal statements of Ezra and Nehemiah. The legal texts (Ezra 10:11, Neh. 10:31, cf. 13:23) specifically state that intermarriage is forbidden regardless of which partner, the male or female, is Jewish. Yet the story (Ezra 9:2,

10:2, 10, cf. Neh. 13:23) relates only to the non-Jewish wives and their offspring. Further, we are told that marriage with a non-Jewish wife leads to the diluting of the "holy seed among the peoples of the land" (Ezra 9:2).

The most likely explanation is that already at this time there was a definite distinction between males and females regarding inter-marriage. Whereas all intermarriages were prohibited, the offspring of Jewish mothers were considered Jewish. The offspring of non-Jewish mothers were not. Hence, the non-Jewish wives and their children were the primary area of concern. It was they who repre-sented the loss of Jewish descent (*zera' ha-qodesh,* Ezra 9:2). Further, Neh. 13:23 once again emphasizes that these children were regarded as not Jewish.[44]

It would seem, then, that the laws expressed in our mishnah and tosefta passages regarding the qualifications of the born or hereditary Jew go back as far as the mid-fifth century B.C.E. Indeed, they are confirmed by Josephus for the late Second Temple period. There is, however, no evidence for such regulations in First Temple times. In fact, it seems that apart from Ammon and Moab, with whom intermarriage was eternally prohibited, Israelites might marry those who sought to become part of the people of Israel provided that the required number of generations had elapsed.[45] No formal conversion was necessary. Because Israel was conceived of as a land-related national entity, an informal system was sufficient. When the exile caused Judaism to adapt to its new, extraterritorial existence, the importance of genealogy and descent increased. This is clearly seen in the views of the editors of Kings, Ezra, and Nehemiah. Hence, it seems that the regulations regarding the deter-mination of Jewish descent enshrined in our tannaitic texts must have originated in the Babylonian exile.

By the time of the rise of Christianity, the *halakhah* clearly defined the Jew by birth as one who was born to a Jewish mother. It was in this light that the Pharisaic-Rabbinic sages would evaluate the Jewish status of the early Jewish Christians, as we shall see as our study progresses. We shall also have to consider the process of conversion to Judaism, for it was ultimately by this yardstick that the new Gentile Christians would be measured by the tannaitic tradition.

III. Conversion to Judaism

Besides being a Jew by birth, one might also become a Jew by conversion, also termed proselytism. The *halakhah* regarding conversion was much more complex than that regarding hereditary Jews, as it was important to ensure that converts were seriously committed to their new faith and that they would be fully absorbed into the Jewish people. We shall see that in legislating the laws of proselytism, Judaism expressed its concept of what Jewish identity meant within the historical context of the Greco-Roman world.[1]

Since Second Temple times, there have been four basic requirements for conversion to Judaism: (1) acceptance of the Torah, (2) circumcision for males, (3) immersion, and (4) sacrifice (no longer required after the destruction).

These requisites are explained in a statement attributed to Rabbi Judah the Prince in *Sifre Be-Midbar* 108:[2]

> Rabbi says: Just as Israel did not enter the covenant except by means of three things—circumcision, immersion, and the acceptance of a sacrifice—so it is the same with the proselytes.

This statement is based on a series of *'aggadot* to the effect that Israel was circumcised shortly before the eating of the first paschal lamb, was immersed, and offered sacrifices in preparation for the giving of the Torah at Mount Sinai.[3] Rabbi Judah the Prince understands the entire conversion procedure as an opportunity for the proselyte to celebrate his own reception of the Torah as Israel did at Mount Sinai, for only through sharing in this historic religious experience could the convert become a Jew.

The conversion procedure and ceremony is described in a long
baraita' in B. Yevamot 47a–b:[4]

> Our Rabbis taught: A proselyte who comes to convert at this time,[5]
> we say to him: "Why did you decide[6] to convert? Do you not know
> that Israel at this time[7] is afflicted, oppressed, downtrodden,[8] and
> rejected, and that tribulations are visited upon them?" If he says, "I
> am aware, but I am unworthy," we accept him immediately, and we
> make known to him[9] a few of the lighter commandments and a few of
> the weightier commandments,[10] and we make known to him the
> penalty for transgression[11] of gleaning (the poor man's share),[12] the
> forgotten (sheaves),[13] the corner,[14] and the poor man's tithe.[15] And
> we make known to him the punishment for violating the command-
> ments. . . . And just as we make known to him the punishment for
> violating the commandments, so we also make known to him the
> reward for their observance[16]. . . . We are not too lengthy with him
> nor are we too detailed. If he accepts (this),[17] we circumcise him
> immediately. . . . Once he has recovered, we immerse him immedi-
> ately. And two scholars[18] stand over him[19] and make known to him
> some of the lighter and some of the weightier commandments. If he
> immersed validly, he is like[20] an Israelite in all matters. (In the case
> of) a woman, women[21] position her in the water up to her neck, and
> two scholars stand outside[22] and make known to her some of the
> lighter commandments and some of the weightier command-
> ments. . . .

From the language of our *baraita'*, with its stress on the persecution and downtrodden nature of Israel, it is most likely to have been
composed in its present form in the aftermath of either the Great
Revolt of 66–74 C.E. or the Bar Kokhba Revolt (132–35 C.E.).
Regardless of which of these two dates is correct, the *baraita'* reflects
the legal rulings prevalent among the tannaim by the Yavnean
period, as will be seen below. That the *baraita'* does not represent the
procedure as followed before 70 C.E. is certain from the absence of
mention of the sacrifice which would have been included had the
Temple cult still been functioning.

Much attention has been paid by scholars to the question of the attitude of the Jews to proselytism. While extended discussion of this question is beyond the scope of this study, one point should be made. The discouragement of would-be proselytes as envisaged in our text is designed to avoid leading them into a spur-of-the-moment decision. Nevertheless, Talmudic sources make clear that the true convert is to be accepted. It is true that for much of Jewish history would-be converts were by and large strongly discouraged. This was for the most part a result of the precarious position of the Jew among his non-Jewish neighbors and of various legal disabilities under which Judaism and conversion were placed, factors beyond the control of the Jewish community.

Acceptance of the Torah

The Torah which the convert had to accept is to be understood in its widest sense. The proselyte must identify fully with the past, present, and future of the Jewish people and live in accord with *halakhah,* the Jewish way of life. The tannaim expected the convert to become part of the nation of Israel and to suffer its collective destiny. It was not, in their view, possible to convert and at the same time to avoid the lot of the Jewish people. Only a convert who understood and was willing to accept the mission of the people of Israel could be accepted for proselytism.

It would have been too much to expect the new convert to master the entirety of the *halakhah* before converting. After all, so much of the practical side of Judaism is learned through experience. For this reason, it was decided that the proselyte would be informed in advance of a sampling of the commandments of the Torah.[23] Of these, some had to be of those easier to fulfill and some of those more difficult. Only in this way could the prospective proselyte properly evaluate the lot he was choosing. He had to understand as well the reward and punishment dimension of the laws for which he would now assume responsibility.

Laws regarding charity for the poor are specifically singled out as the only essential subject of discussion. To the Rabbis, one who did not identify with the Jewish value of *ṣedaqah,* loosely translated as charity, was not ready to become part of the Jewish people. It would not verge on the homiletical to indicate what this shows about the tannaitic view of the importance of sustaining the poor.

That the proselyte's acceptance of the Torah must be total is emphasized in T. Demai 2:5:[24]

> We do not accept a convert who has accepted upon himself all the laws of the Torah except one.[25] Rabbi Yose ben Rabbi Judah says: Even a minor[26] law of the subtleties of the scribes (Rabbinic ordinances).[27]

According to the *baraita'* in B. Yevamot 47a–b, the prospective convert must be told some of the commandments and laws of Judaism. The present passage informs us that if the candidate refuses to accept a law of the Torah (of which he knows), he is to be rejected. The anonymous first clause is taken much further by Rabbi Yose ben Rabbi Judah who says that even if the prospective proselyte rejects only one of the minor Rabbinic ordinances, he is to be disqualified.

Rabbi Yose ben Rabbi Judah's words, if they are in the original form, constitute a gloss to the already formulated first clause. If so, we can assume that the anonymous words of the *baraita'* are to be dated at least as early as the words of Rabbi Yose ben Judah. Unfortunately, this conclusion does not aid us in establishing an early date for the anonymous part of this tosefta. Rabbi Yose ben Judah, son of Judah bar Ilai, was a contemporary of Rabbi Judah the Prince, compiler of the Mishnah.

Comparison should be made here with the famous tannaitic narrative regarding Shammai, Hillel, and the proselyte.[28] The story relates that a non-Jew wanted to convert to Judaism on the condition that he accept only the written and not the oral Law. Shammai rejected him. Hillel convinced him to accept the oral Torah as well.

Regardless of the exact dating of this tradition,[29] or of the dating of the dual-Torah concept as it appears in tannaitic times,[30] it is clear that this *'aggadah* is in agreement with Rabbi Yose ben Judah in that it requires the acceptance of both the oral and written Torah for conversion.

We should note that in the conversions of Helena of Adiabene and her son, Izates (c. 30 C.E.), as described by Josephus in Ant. XX, ii, 3–5 (34–53), instruction in and acceptance of the Torah were part of the conversion process.[31] While we cannot document the requirement of acceptance of the Torah for conversion before 30 C.E., this requirement must have existed from the very beginnings of proselytism in Second Temple times. After all, the institution of conversion was specifically created to allow those who had come to accept Judaism and its Scriptures to enter the Jewish people formally.

Circumcision

From the Pentateuchal references to circumcision (Gen. 17:23–27, Lev. 12:3) it is clear that already in the biblical period circumcision was viewed as a *sine qua non* for Israelite males and for male slaves. The only period for which we have evidence that it was not practiced is that of the wandering in the desert (Josh. 5:2–9). At this time it was probably dispensed with because of the risk it involved.[32]

Circumcision has been customary in many areas of the world. Specifically, Herodotus cites this practice among Egyptians, Syrians, and various peoples in Asia Minor. He attempts to prove that its origin is in Egypt.[33] Evidence points as well to familiarity with circumcision in Canaan, although it is not known in ancient Mesopotamia. The Arabs were already circumcised in the pre-Islamic period. It appears from Jer. 9:24f. that the peoples of Trans-Jordan (Edom, Ammon, and Moab) were also circumcised. On the other hand, the Philistines are denigrated as uncircumcised. Eventually, "uncircumcised" became a term of derision, so that it could be applied even to nations in which it was the usual custom.

The practice of circumcision by non-Jews waned in the Second Temple period, perhaps as a result of Hellenistic influence, and circumcision became the sign of the Jew. Thus Judith 14:10 tells us of the requirement of circumcision for conversion, and 1 Macc. 1:15 relates that those wishing to assimilate and Hellenize attempted to reverse the sign of their circumcision. Jub. 15:33f. accents the importance of this rite as well. When the Seleucids imposed their restrictions on Judaism, they chose, among other things, to prohibit circumcision (1 Macc. 1:60–64).[34]

Greco-Roman sources regarding the Jews uniformly characterize them as circumcised. In fact, the manifold references to this aspect of Judaism show that it was seen by the non-Jew as the distinguishing feature of the Jew. References to it continue unabated throughout the Hellenistic and Roman periods and relate to both Palestinian and Diaspora Jews of both Hebrew and Greek speech and manners.[35]

It was not only under the Seleucids that circumcision became so prominent in the international affairs of the Jews. Circumcision was also outlawed by Hadrian, most probably before the Bar Kokhba rebellion.[36] Indeed, T. Shabbat 15:9 informs us that many practiced epispasm during this period in order to hide their circumcision. This tosefta seems to indicate that during the rebellion, when beyond Roman control, many of these Jews were circumcised again.[37]

Several instances of intermarriage between members of the Herodian household and various aristocratic non-Jews must be noted as well. It was the practice of the Herodians, despite their willingness to otherwise disregard the *halakhah* and its sages, to require circumcision of these "converts."[38] The Herodians knew full well that their only pretext for ruling over the Jews and their land was their questionable claim of Jewish descent. Therefore, they could not dare to intermarry with those not circumcised.

The requirement of circumcision in the conversion process may be clarified by an understanding of its various meanings. Among Jews and Moslems the popular conception is that circumcision renders the boy a member of the religious community. From the biblical point of view, circumcision was a sign of the covenant between God and the descendants of Abraham.[39] In the case of a convert, this rite served as a test of sincerity and dedication. Therefore, it seems most natural that once a conversion procedure developed, it would be incumbent upon the candidate to be circumcised. After all, without circumcision one could not be considered a member of the Jewish people.

Some scholars have claimed that while Palestinian Judaism in the Greco-Roman period required circumcision for proselytism, the Hellenistic Jews did not.[40] Evidence for this theory is extremely weak, especially in light of the widespread perception among the non-Jews at this time that circumcision was the characteristic sign of the Jew.[41]

The story of Ananias and Izates of Adiabene in Ant. XX, ii, 4 (34–48), often cited as proof that Hellenistic Judaism did not require circumcision for conversion, actually proves the reverse. Izates, the young king of Adiabene, had decided to convert to Judaism. He understood entirely that circumcision was required for full-fledged status as a Jew. His mother, Helena, and his teacher, Ananias, feared that Izates' subjects would revolt rather than be ruled by a Jew. Ananias also feared for his life if his role in the affair should be discovered. It was only for this reason that Ananias counseled the king to forgo circumcision and remain a semi-proselyte. Ananias never stated that circumcision was not necessary for a proselyte but rather suggested that the king observe Jewish law without formal conversion.[42]

It is most likely that circumcision was required from the earliest beginnings of the conversion procedure in Second Temple times. However, before the Maccabean Revolt such a requirement cannot be documented, since the Second Temple sources are so very scanty.

Immersion

The requirement of immersion in a ritual bath takes on its greatest significance for the conversion of women. The obligation of circumcision of proselytes only applied to males, and the sacrifice became impossible with the destruction of the Temple. Therefore, for women, from the Yavnean period on, the only requirement besides acceptance of the Torah was immersion.[43]

There is considerable debate about the purpose of the immersion of converts. One point of view is that the immersion serves to purify the proselyte from the impurity of Gentiles. This concept of post-biblical origin was considered a Rabbinic ordinance by the sages.[44] The convert would purify himself in preparation for his new Jewish status. Others have seen the immersion as initiatory, much like Christian baptism, which, most probably, derives from Jewish proselyte immersion.[45]

The Hebrew Bible provides ample background for understanding the requirement as a purification ritual, as such lustrations form a central part of the Israelite cult. On the other hand, the Hebrew Bible provides no basis for understanding this procedure as symbolic of the creation of a new or reborn person, and no reference to such a concept is to be found in the Hebrew Bible, the Apocrypha, Philo, or Josephus. For this reason, some have maintained that this Jewish practice was a result of Christian influence. Nonetheless, prevalent opinion now sees Jewish immersion of proselytes as antedating the Christian usage. It should be noted that there is no evidence of the use of water lustrations for *initiatory* purposes in the Dead Sea Scrolls.[46]

It is probable that the debate as to whether the ritual bath is initiatory or purificatory is best resolved by understanding proselyte immersion as combining both elements.[47] The immersion should be seen as an initiatory rite in which the convert is cleansed of his transgressions and impurities and emerges from the bath as a new person, starting a new life. Since the Christians must have been using the ceremony of baptism as part of their initiation rites at the very least by the time the early New Testament documents were being redacted, we can state with certainty that this practice existed among the Jews at least by the mid-first century C.E. Earlier evidence has been adduced from Rabbinic passages to which we shall turn presently.

M. Pesaḥim 8:8 has been cited as evidence that immersion of proselytes was already practiced in the late first century B.C.E., even before the destruction:[48]

> If a proselyte converted on the day before Passover, the House of Shammai says: He immerses and eats his paschal offering in the evening. But the House of Hillel says: One who departs from (his) foreskin is (as impure) as one who departs from a grave.

This mishnah concerns a convert who was circumcised on the fourteenth of Nisan, the day on which the paschal sacrifice is slaughtered. The House of Shammai says that he is to immerse that day and to eat the paschal sacrifice in the evening. The House of Hillel says that this proselyte should be considered at least as impure as one who had been at a grave and who therefore had contracted the impurity of the dead (cf. Num. 19:18f.). This would mean that following the completion of the conversion (including the immersion), the proselyte would still have to wait seven days and undergo the required ablutions to be cleansed of the impurity of the dead.[49] B. Pesaḥim 92a explains this as a Rabbinic ordinance designed to ensure that the new Jew would not err in future years by thinking that he could purify himself from impurity of the dead in the morning before coming to the Temple and partake of the paschal sacrifice that same evening.[50] A passage in T. Pesaḥim 7:14 supports this interpretation:[51]

> Said Rabbi Eleazar, son of Rabbi Zadok:[52] The House of Shammai and the House of Hillel (both) agree[53] that an uncircumcised male[54] (Jew) receives sprinkling and then eats. Concerning what do they disagree? Regarding an uncircumcised non-Jew. For the House of Shammai says: He immerses and then eats his paschal offering in the evening. But the House of Hillel says: One who departs from (his) foreskin is (as impure) as one who departs from a grave. The law is the same for the non-Jew who was circumcised and the female slave who immersed. Rabbi Eliezer ben Jacob[55] says: There were soldiers[56] and gatekeepers[57] in Jerusalem who immersed and ate their paschal offerings in the evening.

Rabbi Eleazar ben Zadok explains that all agree that in a case in which a Jew is circumcised on the day before Passover, he may be sprinkled in advance. After circumcision, as is known from parallels, he immerses and then may eat of the paschal offering. The disagreement in our mishnah, the Tosefta tells us, concerns only a non-Jew who was circumcised on the day before Passover. The House of Shammai allows him to eat of the paschal offering immediately after his immersion. The House of Hillel regards him as being as impure as if he had contracted the impurity of the dead. He must, therefore, wait the seven-day purification period to be cleansed of impurity of the dead. This is in order to be certain that he will not err in future years and partake of the paschal offering or visit the Temple while in a state of impurity. So the House of Hillel actually required two ablutions, one for conversion and one for purification, while the House of Shammai required only one.

The Tosefta then notes that the House of Hillel takes the same view regarding a handmaiden who has immersed.[58] In order for her to partake of the paschal offering, she must be purified as if she had contracted impurity of the dead.

Finally, to illustrate the view of the Shammaites, Rabbi Eliezer ben Jacob relates that there were Roman soldiers and gatekeepers in Jerusalem who converted and were allowed to eat of the paschal offering after immersion without purification from impurity of the dead. There is no further evidence as to why these Roman soldiers would have decided to convert at the last minute. One may speculate, however, that the pageantry and beauty of the preparations for the paschal sacrifice and the Passover festival enticed them to enter into the Jewish people so as to be able to participate.

This material has been treated at length here in order to clarify a passage which has been treated facilely in some discussions of conversion. It is certain that when the Mishnah and Tosefta refer to immersion[59] here, this is the immersion which was part of the conversion ceremony. When the tannaim wanted to designate the purification from the impurity of the dead which is also required by the Hillelites, it is referred to as sprinkling.[60] It can be stated with certainty, then, that our passage assumes the requirement of immersion for conversion.

How precisely can we date this material? First, the Mishnah and Tosefta concern a dispute of the houses of Hillel and Shammai which must have taken place either while the Temple still stood or in the early Yavnean period. By this time, there is no disagreement at all about the requirement of immersion. Different versions of the *baraita*'[61] place the explanation in the name of Rabbi Eleazar ben Zadok, Rabbi Yose ben Judah, and Rabbi Simeon ben Eleazar. There were two tannaim named Eleazar ben Zadok. It is probable that we are dealing here with the latter. Nonetheless, it should be remembered that he lived during the Temple period and related things about the Temple in his teachings. Rabbi Yose ben Judah is a contemporary of Rabbi Judah the Prince, redactor of the Mishnah. The statement also appears in B. Pesaḥim 92a in the name of Rabbi Simeon ben Eleazar, a pupil of Rabbi Meir and contemporary of Judah the Prince.

On the one hand, we have failed to establish a definite attestation of our tradition at an early date. On the other hand, the transmission of this statement in the names of three separate tannaim indicates that it was widespread, and we may therefore take it as reliable evidence that the dispute of the Hillelites and Shammaites circulated from the Yavnean period on in the schools of the tannaim.

Rabbi Eliezer ben Jacob supports the Shammaite view. Lieberman sees him as the second rabbi of this name, the contemporary of Rabbi Meir. In any case, we have further evidence for this discussion in the tannaitic period when there is no doubt that immersion is required.

What can now be said about the evidence for the dating of immersion as a requirement for conversion? First, it seems that it is necessary to date it before the time of John the Baptist and the rise of Christianity in order to understand the background against which baptism comes to the fore. Second, tannaitic evidence, although admittedly lacking early attestation, also lends support to the claim that immersion was already a necessary requirement for conversion in late Second Temple times. Nonetheless, we cannot prove that immersion was a *sine qua non* for conversion before the early first century C.E.[62]

Sacrifice

Regarding the sacrificial offering which a convert must bring, M. Keritot 2:1 states:[63]

> Four are lacking in atonement . . . the gonorrheac,[64] the woman with extra-menstrual bleeding,[65] the woman who gave birth, and the *meṣora'*.[66] Rabbi Eliezer ben Jacob says: The proselyte is lacking in atonement until the blood is sprinkled on his behalf, and the Nazirite (is also lacking in atonement). . . .

"Lacking in atonement" is a technical term for those who have completed the prescribed purification ritual, including immersion, but are still not permitted to partake of sacrifices until they have brought an offering and its blood has been sprinkled on the altar. The use of the word *kippurim*, "atonement," in this way does not imply sin or the need for any form of forgiveness.[67] Rather, the term is used here in a technical sense devoid of its usual connotation.[68]

The Mishnah presents a list of those falling into this category. Rabbi Eliezer ben Jacob modifies the anonymous list of the first clause by adding two more cases, one of which is the proselyte.

There is no question that a proselyte must bring an offering before he may eat of other sacrifices. The debate concerns the reason for this offering. The anonymous part of the mishnah takes the view that the sacrifice is a part of the initiatory conversion rites and, therefore, that until it is offered the convert is not a Jew and may not eat of the sacrifices. Hence, the convert does not fit the classification of the "one lacking in atonement."

To Rabbi Eliezer ben Jacob, the main purpose of the sacrifice is one of purification (or atonement), and hence he sees the convert as fully Jewish without the sacrifice. The offering, in his view, is necessary only to purify him so that he may now eat of the sacrifices. For this reason he adds the proselyte to the list of those "lacking in atonement."

In the view of B. Keritot 2b, reference to "four" who "are lacking in atonement" specifically excludes the case of the proselyte. If this interpretation is correct, the practice of the convert's sacrifice can be dated as early as the anonymous mishnah. On the other hand, it is possible that it was only discussed in the days of Rabbi Eliezer ben Jacob whose view regarding the proselyte was rejected by the sages of his time. Nevertheless, we can deduce from this mishnah that by the time of Rabbi Eliezer ben Jacob there was no disagreement about the necessity for the convert to bring a sacrifice, only about the specific reason for this requirement.

It appears from the attribution to Rabbi Eliezer ben Jacob that the tradition dates back to Temple times. Scholars have concluded that there were two Rabbis Eliezer ben Jacob, the earlier of whom lived before the destruction of the Second Temple.[69] Since many of his teachings (including an early recension of the tractate Middot) dealt with the Temple and its cult, it is most likely that he is the author of our tradition.[70]

The requirement of a sacrifice must have been in force while the Temple stood. But how far back can it be established? From M. Keritot 2:1 we can date the practice to the last years of the Second Temple. It seems from Josephus (Ant. XX, iii, 5 [49]) that after Helena of Adiabene converted to Judaism (her immersion is not mentioned), she went to Jerusalem to offer a sacrifice. If this sacrifice was a conversion offering, it would date our practice to as early as c. 30 C.E.[71]

The problem of what would be done about the sacrifice after the destruction of the Temple in 70 C.E. was dealt with immediately. A *baraita'* in B. Keritot 9a reads:[72]

Our Rabbis taught: A proselyte at this time[73] must set aside a fourth (dinar)[74] for his pair (of sacrificial birds). Said Rabbi Simeon:[75] Rabban Yoḥanan ben Zakkai already resolved to eliminate it[76] (the setting aside of money) because of the danger of error.

The first clause of the *baraita'* is anonymous and clearly reflects the view taken in the immediate aftermath of the destruction. It states that it is obligatory for the proselyte, even in the absence of the Temple, to set aside the money to pay for his sacrificial offering; for, as Rashi explains, the Temple may be rebuilt and then he would be able to offer his sacrifice. Nevertheless, we are told that Rabban Yoḥanan ben Zakkai at Yavneh, soon after the destruction, negated this practice to avoid the possibility that the money would be used by accident for some other purpose and the proselyte would be guilty of misappropriation of funds dedicated for Temple sacrifices.

The abolition of this practice by Rabban Yoḥanan ben Zakkai is mentioned in a statement attributed to Rabbi Simeon. Normally, we would assume that this is Rabbi Simeon ben Yoḥai who lived at the time of the Bar Kokhba Revolt. However, a parallel text in B. Rosh Ha-Shanah 31b states it in the name of Rabbi Simeon ben Eleazar,[77] a slightly later tanna who was a contemporary of Rabbi Judah the Prince. It is unfortunate that we do not have an earlier attribution for the elimination of this practice by Yoḥanan ben Zakkai. Therefore, we cannot be entirely certain if he did eliminate it, or if in an effort to justify its elimination in the second century, the tannaim appealed to his authority to strengthen their argument.

Thus far, the principal sources relating to the requirements of conversion have been investigated. Careful attention has been paid to the dating of the sources as well as of the practices they describe. We have concluded that circumcision and the acceptance of the Torah must have been part of the ceremony from its earliest date in Second Temple times. For immersion, we cannot prove that it was practiced for proselytes before the early first century C.E. In regard to the sacrifice, it was certainly offered in the early first century C.E.

A Later Tannaitic Controversy

Several *baraitot* attributed to sages in the late first or second century might seem at first glance to contradict the dating proposed here for the various requirements of the conversion ceremony. It is therefore necessary to analyze these passages. Specifically, we shall examine a *baraita'* appearing in two versions (with significant variation) in the Palestinian and Babylonian Talmuds, and a *baraita'* taught by a Palestinian amora[78] which appears in connection with the first *baraita'*.

The *baraita'* as it appears in B. Yevamot 46a is as follows:[79]

> Our Rabbis taught: If a proselyte was circumcised but did not immerse, Rabbi Eliezer says that indeed this is a (valid) proselyte, for thus we have found regarding our fathers,[80] that they were circumcised but did not immerse. If he (the proselyte) immersed but was not circumcised, Rabbi Joshua says that indeed this is a (valid) proselyte. For thus we have found regarding our mothers, that they immersed but were not circumcised. But the sages say: If he (the proselyte) immersed but was not circumcised, (or) was circumcised but did not immerse, he is not a (valid) proselyte until he is circumcised and immerses.

The version of the *baraita'* found in P. Qiddushin 3:12 (3:14, 64d) is considerably different:[81]

> (A tanna) taught: If a proselyte was circumcised but did not immerse, or immersed and was not circumcised, the entire matter is dependent upon the circumcision. These are the words of Rabbi Eliezer. Rabbi Joshua[82] says: Even the (lack of) immersion renders it (the conversion) invalid.

In contradistinction to this *baraita'*, the Palestinian gemara then quotes a second *baraita'* taught by an amora:[83]

> Bar Kappara taught: A proselyte who was circumcised but did not immerse[84] is indeed a fit (proselyte), for there is no proselyte who has not immersed[85] because of his seminal emissions.[86]

Rabbi Eliezer of our controversy is Rabbi Eliezer ben Hyrcanus, and Rabbi Joshua is Joshua ben Hananiah. Both men were leading sages of the period between the Great Revolt (66–74 C.E.) and the Bar Kokhba revolution (132–35 C.E.). The controversy recorded here is ascribed, therefore, to the late first or early second century C.E.

In other words, the debates recorded here occurred some time after we have maintained that the essential requirements were already fixed beyond dispute. Some scholars have sought to use these sources to show that, in fact, the dispute over the essential requirements of conversion was not settled as early as proposed here.[87] Yet a correct understanding of the traditions will show that there was by this time no dispute regarding the requirements for conversion.

Comparison of the Palestinian and Babylonian versions shows some confusion about the views of the various tannaim. In the Babylonian version, Rabbi Eliezer makes circumcision the *sine qua non,* accepting as valid the proselyte who has not undergone immersion. Rabbi Joshua takes the opposite view and sees immersion as the *sine qua non.* In his view, the convert can be considered a Jew even without circumcision.[88] It is the view of the sages that both immersion and circumcision are essential for male converts.[89]

The Palestinian version ascribes to Rabbi Eliezer the view that the *sine qua non* is circumcision and that immersion is not essential. Here, however, Rabbi Joshua is seen as taking the view that *both* circumcision and immersion are absolute requirements, this view having been ascribed to the sages in the Babylonian version.

The difference between the Babylonian and Palestinian versions is explained by D. Halivni[90] as having arisen in the following manner: Originally, the view of Rabbi Eliezer was recorded to the effect that circumcision was decisive. To this was added Rabbi Joshua's view that "the (lack of) immersion renders it (the conversion) invalid."[91] Rabbi Joshua meant to say that the only *sine qua non* is the immersion. The redactor of the *baraita'* in the Palestinian version understood Rabbi Joshua to say that *both* circumcision and immersion are required. Accordingly, the redactor added "even"[92] in order to clarify matters. In so doing, he misconstrued the words of Rabbi Joshua and brought about the contradiction between the Palestinian and Babylonian versions.

It must be noted that the view of Bar Kappara in the Palestinian amoraic *baraita'* is almost identical to that of the sages in the Babylonian version. The sages require both circumcision and immersion, and Bar Kappara agrees that both are absolutely essential. Bar Kappara, however, thinks that the requirement of immersion, if omitted, can be considered fulfilled, since all proselytes would begin immersing regularly after assuming the obligations of a Jew.[93]

One other major difference exists between the Babylonian and Palestinian versions. The Babylonian version contains an explanation of the reasons for the views of Rabbi Eliezer and Rabbi Joshua. Indeed, it is these explanations which the gemara immediately comments upon in analyzing this *baraita'*.[94] The absence of these explanations in the Palestinian version would lead us to believe that it probably represents an earlier recension.[95]

The Babylonian version of the *baraita'* states the reasoning behind the views of Rabbi Eliezer and Rabbi Joshua. The opinion of the sages is not followed by an explanation. Therefore, it is most likely that the sages' view was originally formulated separately from the views of Rabbi Eliezer and Rabbi Joshua and then attached to them.[96]

Now let us return to the basic issue posed by these *baraitot*. Is it possible, despite all the evidence we have marshaled so far, that as late as the turn of the first century C.E. the sages would consider the possibility that one could enter the Jewish people with the omission of either circumcision or immersion? Indeed, one might be tempted to see here the source of the Christian rejection of circumcision and acceptance of baptism as a sufficient rite for entry into the Church.

Nonetheless, the correct view is undoubtedly that of B. Bamberger.[97] He explains the argument as a technical dispute regarding the precise point in the process of conversion at which the proselyte may be considered a Jew. Is the act of circumcision or that of immersion the decisive factor? Can a proselyte who has only undergone one of these rites be considered a full-fledged Jew before completing the ceremonies?

Behind this dispute is a larger question. Which rite is the actual conversion rite? Should it be understood that circumcision is the final step, with immersion only a halakhic requirement which the new Jew must fulfill to purify himself of the impurity of the Gentiles? Or, on the other hand, is immersion the actual conversion rite and the proselyte now obligated, like any other Jew, to be circumcised? Finally, the third view is simply that both are essential parts of the conversion process.

The disputes under discussion, then, are best understood as technical, Rabbinic debates regarding the exact point at which the proselyte becomes a full-fledged Jew. They cannot be seen as evidence for essential disagreements regarding the conversion procedure or its requirements.

'Eved Kena'ani

The converts spoken about thus far have been free men who have decided of their own free will to join the Jewish people and to accept Judaism. There was, however, another type of convert, the 'eved kena'ani, literally the "Canaanite slave" but designating all non-Jewish slaves.[98]

When non-Jewish slaves were bought, they were to be circumcised in accordance with the law of Gen. 17:12f. (cf. Ex. 12:44). Slaves refusing to be circumcised were to be resold to Gentiles, although prevalent tannaitic opinion allowed a twelve-month period for convincing the slave to undergo circumcision. In addition, the new slave was immersed. These rites qualified him fully as a Jew in all matters, and his status regarding observance of the commandments was the same as that of women. The common denominator was that women and slaves were exempt from commandments with specific time requirements because they were not in control of their own use of time.

If the master wanted to free his slave, a practice encouraged by the tannaim, the slave was again immersed and given a writ of manumission. He was now a free Jew with a status similar to that of a convert.[99]

Later authorities rightly assume that the procedures followed in regard to proselytes were also followed for "Canaanite" slaves.[100] Thus, before immersion, the slave had to be familiarized with the commandments and had to indicate his assent. Further, although the sources are silent here, it is possible that a newly freed slave after his immersion (for the purpose of initiation as a free man) would have brought the same sacrifice as the convert.

While undoubtedly the origins of these laws lie in forced conversion of captives and slaves, by tannaitic times only those who freely accepted Judaism and circumcision could go through the rituals. On the other hand, there is no question that the Hasmonean kings practiced forced conversions,[101] and it is possible that private individuals in the Hasmonean period also forced their slaves to accept Judaism and to be circumcised.

Semi-Proselytes

The proselytes described above have been those who joined the Jewish people by following the procedures mandated by the *halakhah* and became full members of the Jewish community. Hellenistic and Rabbinic sources, regarding both Palestine and the Diaspora during the Greco-Roman period, tell us of semi-proselytes or God-fearers who attached themselves to the Jewish people. Apparently, as a result of the general interest in Oriental religions and of the waning of the old Greco-Roman cults, many people in the Hellenistic world were attracted to various Jewish customs, including the Sabbath, synagogue attendance, and abstention from pork, among other things. Some went so far as to adopt almost all Jewish practices as well as the ethics and theology of Judaism. On the other hand, these people never underwent actual conversion. We know that in some cases, this was because of the requirement of circumcision. In other cases, family members or fear of public embarrassment prevented actual proselytism. Such God-fearers or semi-proselytes were found throughout the Hellenistic world in substantial numbers, and it may be that the Jewish community actually encouraged this behavior, especially in the Diaspora.[102]

Nevertheless, these people had no legal status in the Jewish community, whether in Palestine or elsewhere. They were not converts, regardless of the extent of their loyalty. Only the fulfillment of the requirements of conversion, which, as far as we know, were agreed upon by all Jews, would allow entrance to the Jewish people. Apparently, these semi-proselytes did not desire legal status within the Jewish community. Their practices differed, and they were in no way organized or united. While many Jews approved of such individuals, they could never conceive of them as Jews since they had not undergone formal conversion.

Jewish Self-Definition in Tannaitic Sources

Since the tannaitic sources regarding the hereditary or born Jew and the means of entering the Jewish people by conversion have been thoroughly investigated, it ought to be possible to extract from them some significant findings regarding the self-image and self-definition of the tannaitic Jewish community.[103] Such conclusions ought to serve us well when we consider early Christianity in the context of tannaitic thought as expressed in the *halakhah*.

To begin with, Judaism is centered on the Jewish people, a group whose membership is fundamentally determined by heredity. If one is not born a Jew, how can one become a Jew? Here the *halakhah* demands the maximum of commitment, for the convert is literally changing his heredity. He will pass on to his children descent which he did not inherit but rather acquired. For this reason, he must undergo an extensive procedure in order to acquire fully the main characteristics of what Jewishness is.

He must be committed to the acceptance of the Torah. He himself must stand at Sinai, for Sinai was the formative event in the Jewish historical experience. There he, like the people of ancient Israel, must accept not only the laws of the Torah but also the Rabbinic interpretation or oral Law which, in the view of the tannaim, was given at Sinai as well.

He must also identify with the entire historic experience of the Jews. He must understand that his fate is now linked with that of his new coreligionists, for he has literally switched his heredity to become part of the Jewish people. He must at the same time acquire the characteristic of charity and kindness which Jews have been proud to maintain.

The male convert must be circumcised, for this is considered the ultimate sign of Jewish identity and of the covenant in which he is now enrolling. Even more important, he is to become a descendant of Abraham, and the Torah has commanded that Abraham's descendants be circumcised.

He must purify himself in a ritual bath, for the Jewish people saw itself, from its earliest origins, as striving to live a life of purity and holiness. How else but in absolute holiness could one receive the Torah and enter into membership in the kingdom of priests?

Finally, he must bring a sacrifice, an act which receives the assent of God, for without God's favor and acceptance, no Jew could sustain himself. In bringing the sacrifice, he shows that he is ready to draw near to the divine presence and to come under its wings as a full member of the people of Israel.

Based on the foregoing discussion, it is now certain that the *halakhot* regarding the identity of the Jew by birth and the procedure for conversion to Judaism were in force before the rise of Christianity. The Rabbis, we shall see, would apply these rules to the determination of the identity of the early Christians, both Jewish and Gentile, and to the question of whether Christianity was to be regarded as a Jewish sect or a separate religion. Yet before proceeding to the historical questions before us, we shall have to investigate the tannaitic traditions pertaining to heretics and apostates to see if these categories might have led the tannaim to any conclusions regarding the status of the early Christians.

IV. Heretics and Apostates

Thus far the definitions of the born Jew and the convert have been established for the period immediately preceding and contemporaneous with the rise of Christianity. What must be asked now is whether one can be excluded from the Jewish people and lose his Jewish status as a result of any beliefs or actions. Indeed, it will be shown conclusively that this cannot occur and that only the criteria described above could serve to indicate who was or was not a Jew in the early centuries of this era.

A word of definition is in order. A heretic is one whose *beliefs* do not accord with those of the established religion to which he claims adherence. An apostate is one whose *actions* are not consonant with the standards of behavior set by his religious community. We shall have to treat these classes separately, as they involve different halakhic categories.

Heresy

The starting point for any discussion of heresy in tannaitic Judaism must be the *locus classicus* of M. Sanhedrin 10:1:[1]

> The following[2] are those who do not have a portion[3] in the world to come:[4] the one who says there is no resurrection of the dead,[5] (the one who says) the Torah is not from heaven, and the *'apiqoros*.[6]

It is this passage which has served as the basis of most claims that Judaism has a creed.[7] This mishnah effectively suggests that those who hold certain beliefs are excluded from the world to come, and that opposite beliefs are normative and required.[8] We shall investi-

gate the specific offenses mentioned and show that exclusion from a
portion in the world to come does not imply expulsion from the
Jewish people.

The case of one who does not believe in the world to come is
explained in a *baraita'* in B. Sanhedrin 90a:[9]

> (A tanna taught): He denied resurrection of the dead. Therefore, he
> will not have a portion in the resurrection of the dead.[10] For all the
> retributions of the Holy One, Blessed be He, are measure for
> measure. . . .[11]

This *baraita'* is noteworthy in that it indicates that the tannaim
understood the phrase "world to come" as it appears in our mishnah to refer to the period after the resurrection of the dead. For this
reason, the *baraita'* substituted the term "resurrection of the dead"
for "world to come" in recapitulating the content of the mishnah.
From M. Sanhedrin 10:3 we learn that after resurrection there will
be divine judgment followed by the world to come. The *baraita'*
explains that since the person in question denied the existence of the
resurrection of the dead, he will be denied the right to be resurrec-
ted. Accordingly, he will not attain a portion in the world to come.

This mishnah is most probably directed against the Sadducees,
who, Josephus tells us, did not accept either the immortality of the
soul or the idea of reward and punishment after death.[12] Indeed,
both of these doctrines are inextricably connected with the doctrine
of resurrection as mentioned in our mishnah, and the Pharisees saw
resurrection as a prelude to the world to come. Our mishnah states
that those Sadducees who deny resurrection of the dead would
therefore have no share in the world to come.[13]

The second class of non-believers are those who deny the
heavenly or divine origin of the Torah. It might be tempting to view
the Torah here as a reference to *torah she-be-'al peh,* the oral Law,
which the tannaim believed was given to Moses on Sinai along with
the written Torah. (Indeed, this meaning might perhaps be attributed as well to the statement of M. 'Avot 1:1 that "Moses received the

Torah from Sinai.") Unfortunately, we cannot date the use of the term "oral Law" any earlier than the Yavnean period.[14] Since, as will be shown below, it is likely that this mishnah predates the destruction of the Temple, the term "Torah" here may be limited in meaning to the written Law.[15] The person described by our mishnah, therefore, denies the prophetic character of Moses and, in effect, asserts that Moses himself was the author of the Pentateuch.

It is known from Greco-Roman sources that some classical authors attacked the Torah, claiming that Moses had made it up and that he had ascribed divine authorship to it only in order to assure observance of its laws. Indeed, from Philo of Alexandria and from some much later midrashic sources it seems that some Jews came to believe the same thing.[16] In fact, it is probable that those who wished to substitute the constitution of the Greek polis for that of the Torah in Hellenistic Jerusalem did so out of belief that both were man-made, whereas the polis offered greater possibilities for advancement, both economic and political.[17] It is most likely that our mishnah is directed against those who, perhaps under Hellenistic influence, had come to deny the divine origin of the Torah. They, therefore, are a class who will not share in the world to come.

How did the Rabbis arrive at such a conclusion? The case of the denial of resurrection was understood by the tannaim as based on the doctrine of equivalent recompense ("measure for measure"). The same doctrine must have motivated the Rabbis here. The promise of ultimate bliss in the world to come after resurrection and divine judgment is meant as a reward for observance of the commandments. For Jews this means observance of all the commandments of the Torah. For non-Jews it is sufficient to observe the Noachide laws. Only one who accepts the premise on which the entire system of the commandments is based, the divine origin of the Law, can be worthy of receiving the reward which the life of Torah is meant to assure. Hence, he who denies the divine character of the Law cannot reap its rewards.

The third class excluded for reasons of belief from the world to come is the *'apiqoros*. There can be no question of the derivation of this word from the Greek 'Επίκουρος,[18] the name of the famous Greek philosopher Epicurus (342/1–270 B.C.E.). The only question is whether this term signifies a follower of this philosopher or if in Rabbinic literature it has somehow become a more general term for a heretic. The Talmudic definitions of this word,[19] which are based on a Semitic derivation,[20] are amoraic and clearly do not reflect the actual tannaitic usage.

Josephus mentions Epicureans in his discussion of the Book of Daniel.[21] There he says that Daniel's correct prophecies show that the Epicureans who deny providence and assert that the world is without a "ruler and provider"[22] are in error. In other words, to Josephus the Epicurean is one who denies God and His role in the world. It can be assumed that Josephus is using the term "Epicurean" in the way it was understood by the people of his day. The chronological proximity of the mishnah under discussion to the works of Josephus would lead us to the conclusion that the meaning of 'apiqoros in our mishnah is one who denies God's involvement in the affairs of men and the world.

Why did the 'apiqoros lose his portion? Indeed, he denied the very basis of the resurrection, divine judgment, and the world to come. For he denied the role of God, even the concern of God, for the affairs of mankind. Hence, he was unworthy to share in the blessings which God had stored up for mankind in the end of days. Again we find the principle of "measure for measure."

Against whom were the Rabbis polemicizing when they excluded the 'apiqoros from the world to come? According to Josephus, the very same beliefs ascribed to the 'apiqoros were held by the Sadducees.[23] Now it must again be remembered that Josephus wrote at a time not so far from the composition of this mishnaic statement, and so his descriptions of the Sadducees may be taken as accurate for the last days of the Temple. Of course, one must never forget the tendency of Josephus to picture the Jewish sects as if they were Greek philosophic schools.[24] Nevertheless, Josephus does testify to an affinity between the views of the Sadducees and the Epicureanism of the very same period. If so, it is safe to conclude that the 'apiqoros of our mishnah was often a member of the Sadducean group.

We have found that this mishnah describes three forms of heresy, two of which are attributed by Josephus to the Sadducees. Indeed, we must conclude that this mishnah is Pharisaic in origin and polemicized against the Sadducees and certain Hellenized Jews. At the same time, anyone holding these views, regardless of his affiliation with one of the prevalent groups of the Second Temple period, was considered to have lost his portion in the world to come.

Can the statement under discussion be dated?[25] We have so far omitted from discussion the second part of this mishnah, in which Rabbi Akiva and Abba Saul add to the list several heterodox *practices* (as opposed to beliefs dealt with in the anonymous first half of the mishnah) which also exclude the transgressor from the world to come.

The qualitative difference between the offenses of creed listed in the anonymous first part of the mishnah and the offenses of practice listed in the sections attributed to Rabbi Akiva and Abba Saul would tend to support the idea that the original teaching was composed at a time when issues of belief were central. However, in the Yavnean period (the time of Rabbi Akiva and Abba Saul) there was an attempt to strengthen and standardize practice in order to close ranks and to ensure the survival of Judaism in the aftermath of the destruction of the nation and its Temple.[26]

Further, we have seen that the heresies catalogued by this mishnah can all be attributed to or connected with the Sadducees or the Hellenized Jews. It is therefore most probable that the anonymous first clause of the mishnah was composed before the destruction of the Temple while Sadduceeism and Hellenism were still issues for the Pharisaic leaders. After all, the Sadducees were to disappear soon after the destruction with the removal of their power base, the central sanctuary in Jerusalem.

Can it be determined from the material presented thus far whether loss of one's portion in the world to come implies also loss of one's status in the Jewish people or whether the status of a Jew is inviolable regardless of his beliefs? One thing is certain. No intrinsic link can be claimed between Jewish status and the possession of a portion in the world to come. M. Sanhedrin 10:3, for example,

indicates that the men of Sodom have no portion in the world to
come. If a portion in the world to come went hand in hand with
Jewish status, why even mention the men of Sodom? Indeed, T.
Sanhedrin 13:2 contains a tannaitic debate about whether the righteous of the nations of the world can have a portion in the world to
come. Again, the question of Jewish status and that of a portion in
the world to come are separate issues. The fact that certain heretics
or non-believers are excluded from the world to come in no way
implies expulsion from the Jewish people.

Apostasy

Thus far, the offenses which disqualified a person from a portion
in the world to come were doctrinal. The Tosefta, however, adds
several offenses of commission. The context is a statement attributed
to the House of Shammai in which three classes are delineated:
those righteous receiving immediate reward; the average people,
who will be punished and then receive their reward; and the worst
offenders, who will be consigned permanently to purgatory. T.
Sanhedrin 13:5 concerns this last group:[27]

> But as to the heretics (*minin*),[28] the apostates (*meshummadin*), the
> informers, the *'apiqorsim,* those who have denied the Torah, those
> who have separated from the ways of the community,[29] those who
> have denied the resurrection of the dead,[30] and everyone who has
> transgressed and caused the public to transgress . . .,[31] Gehenna[32] is
> shut in their faces (or "before them"), and they are punished in it
> (Gehenna) for ever and ever.

It is easy to see that this passage represents an expansion of the list
found in the Mishnah, adding certain offenders whose transgressions had such major consequences as to cause the loss of their
portion in the world to come and to bring upon them eternal
punishment.

Min in this context probably means an early Christian. This term as well as the halakhic status of this group will be treated in detail below. Suffice it to say, that according to our passage they are to be subjected to eternal punishment after death.

While the role of informers in Talmudic literature is in need of a thorough study, at least it can be observed that these people denounced Jews who practiced rituals forbidden during the Hadrianic persecutions and perhaps at other times as well.[33] Such denunciations were extremely dangerous to the Jewish community. For this reason, potential informers were threatened with loss of their share in the world to come in order to deter them from committing this offense.

The term *meshummad*[34] is usually translated as "apostate." While this English word denotes one who forsakes his religion, the Hebrew term is more complex. Literally, it means one who has been destroyed. We will see that it refers to one who ignores the commands of the Torah and the demands of Jewish law. According to S. Lieberman,[35] the term originally referred to one forced to worship idols and only later came to refer to one who committed offenses of his own free will. In any case, this wider meaning is already represented in the tannaitic sources before us.

The distinction between the *meshummad le-te'avon,* one who apostasizes for desire of forbidden pleasures, and the *meshummad le-hakh'is,* one who does so out of spite, is an amoraic distinction. Tannaitic *halakhah* displayed an ambivalent attitude toward the apostate who was on different occasions treated with varying degrees of severity. This ambivalence was explained in amoraic times by the assumption that there were two different types of *meshummad* and that they acted out of different motives.

Only two tannaitic passages can be presented in an attempt to reach a more exact definition of the *meshummad.* An anonymous *baraita'* in B. Horayot 11a attempts to define which commandments are such that their violation labels the offender a *meshummad:*[36]

> Our Rabbis taught: If one ate forbidden fat, he is a *meshummad.* And who is a *meshummad?* One who ate [37] animals not ritually slaughtered

or afflicted with fatal diseases,[38] forbidden animals and reptiles,[39] or who drank the wine of (idolatrous) libation. Rabbi Yose, son of Rabbi Judah,[40] says: even one who wears a garment of wool and linen.[41]

This *baraita'* represents the conflation of two sections. The first was an anonymous *baraita'* indicating that one who ate forbidden fat was a *meshummad*. The second asked the question of who was a *meshummad* and answered that one who ate certain forbidden foods fell into this category.[42] To this anonymous definition was added a dictum in the name of Rabbi Yose, son of Rabbi Judah, to the effect that the wearing of *sha'aṭnez,* a garment of mixed wool and linen, also qualified the offender as a *meshummad*.

Rabbi Yose, son of Rabbi Judah, is a late tanna, a contemporary of Rabbi Judah the Prince. We have no way of asserting that even the anonymous clauses of the *baraita'* are earlier than the last days of the tannaitic period, although no evidence against an early date can be marshaled either.

This definition of a *meshummad* is clearly halakhic in character and sees the *meshummad* as one who violated certain dietary restrictions. Indeed, even one who wears mixed linen and wool, in the view of one late tanna, is a member of this class.

A more general definition is found in a *midrash halakhah* based on Lev. 1:2. The version in the *Sifra'* is as follows:[43]

> (Speak to the Children of Israel and say to them: When any of you presents an offering of cattle to the Lord. . . .) Any: to include the proselytes. Of you: to exclude the *meshummadim* . . . . The text (of the Torah) says Children of Israel. . . . Just as Israel are those who have accepted the covenant, so also the proselytes are those who have accepted the covenant. But the *meshummadim* are excluded since they do not accept the covenant.[44] For indeed, they have declared the covenant void. . . .

This statement sees the *meshummad* as the opposite of the proselyte. While the proselyte has undergone acceptance of the Torah as part of the conversion process, the *meshummad* has denied that very covenant.

B. Ḥullin 5a contains a version of this halakhic exegesis which is more expansive:[45]

> Of you:[46] Not all of you, excluding the *meshummad*. Of you: Among
> you (Israel) have I made a distinction but not among the nations. Of
> cattle: to include people who are likened[47] to cattle.[48] From this they
> said,[49] it is permitted to accept sacrifices from the transgressors of
> Israel[50] in order that through them they may come to repent, except
> from the *meshummad* or from one who pours (idolatrous) libations or
> violates the Sabbath in public.

Now this *midrash halakhah* is germane to the central issue: Is the
meshummad considered part of the people of Israel? The *midrash*
answers in the affirmative. Whereas all non-Jews (including
idolators) may send voluntary offerings to be sacrificed in the
Jerusalem Temple, this right is denied to certain Jews, namely to
those who have apostasized to the extent of performing idolatrous
worship or violating the Sabbath in public. These *meshummadim* are,
therefore, still Jews, for if they were excluded from the Jewish
people, their offerings *would* be acceptable. Indeed, this principle is
seen by the tannaim as derived from the Torah itself. There can be
no question, therefore, that the *meshummad,* like the heretic and the
'apiqoros, is never deprived of his Jewish status.[51]

V. Tannaitic Judaism and the Early Christians

It is time to pause to consider the implications for the Jewish-Christian schism of the tannaitic sources studied thus far. The halakhic definitions of a Jew in the pre-Christian era have been established: ancestry through the mother or conversion, including circumcision for males, immersion, acceptance of the Torah, and offering of a sacrifice. These continued to be the only possible ways to enter the Jewish people in the period in which Christianity came to the fore. Further, it was determined that the tannaim did not view heresy or apostasy in and of itself as negating the offender's status as a Jew. Indeed, Jewish status could never be canceled, even for the most heinous offenses against Jewish law and doctrine. It is against this background that the tannaitic reaction to the rise of Christianity must be viewed.

While our sources point to general adherence to Jewish law and practice by the earliest Christians, we must also remember that some deviance from the norms of the tannaim must have occurred already at the earliest period. Indeed, the sayings attributed by the Gospels to Jesus would lead us to believe that he may have taken a view of the *halakhah* that was different from that of the Pharisees. Nonetheless, from the point of view of the halakhic material discussed thus far, the tannaim did not see the earliest Christians as constituting a separate religious community.

Even if we were to accept many of the polemical statements in our sources at face value and assume the violations of *halakhah* in the early Christian community to be more extensive, the early Christians would still be considered Jews. Nor should we assume that the claims that Jesus was a miracle worker or magician, a view encountered so often in the earliest Jewish anti-Christian polemics,[1] would have in any way reflected on the Jewish status of his followers. Even the belief in the divinity or Messiahship of Jesus, as we have seen in our discussion of heresy, would not, in the view of the tannaim, have read the early Christians out of the Jewish community.[2] On the contrary, Judaism had long been accustomed to tolerating both differences of opinion and deviation from the norms of observance by its members.

Indeed, the existence of all kinds of sects and religious leaders was common in the Second Temple period as we know from so many sources. Judaism was in what we might call an experimental stage. The biblical tradition was being adapted in many different ways in an unconscious effort to see which approach would best ensure the future of Judaism and of the Jewish people. For this reason, little opposition to the very concept of sectarian divergence existed. Each group argued for its own primacy and superiority, yet no voice called for the unity of the people as a virtue in and of itself. It was in such a context that Christianity arose. It was seen by the tannaim in its earliest stages as no greater a threat than any other sect, and the halakhic regulations discussed above determined the identity of the early Christians as Jews.

This situation changed with the destruction of the Temple. Divisions within the people, after all, had made the orderly prosecution of the war against the Romans and the defense of the Holy City impossible.[3] The Temple had fallen as a result.[4] Only in unity could the people and the land be rebuilt. It was only a question of which of the sects would unify the populace.

For all intents and purposes, the Pharisees were the only sect to survive the destruction. The smaller sects were either scattered or destroyed. The Sadducees, once in control of the Temple, had been deprived of their base of power and authority with its destruction, and of their status by the social and economic upheaval wrought by the war. This was clearly the time for the entire nation to unite behind the tannaim, the heirs to the Pharisaic approach to Judaism. For Pharisaism, with its flexibility in applying the *halakhah* to new circumstances, would be best fit to deal with the new realities after the unsuccessful revolt and the resulting destruction of the Temple.

But where would the Christians fit into this newly constituted Jewish community? The evidence indicates that the Christians, although still Jewish, had only moderate success in winning converts among the Jews of Palestine.[5] At the same time, the nascent Church turned more and more to Gentiles as prospective converts.[6] Undoubtedly, some of the new converts were Hellenistic Jews for whom the new religion seemed but a variety of Judaism. On the other hand, the vast majority of the new Christians consisted of Gentiles and the former semi-proselytes.

Of the vast numbers of Greco-Roman non-Jews who were attracted to Christianity, only a small number ever became proselytes to Judaism. The new Christianity was primarily Gentile, for it did not require its adherents to become circumcised and convert to Judaism or to observe the Law. Yet at the same time, Christianity in the Holy Land was still strongly Jewish.[7]

As the destruction of the Temple was nearing, the differences between Judaism and Christianity were widening. By the time the Temple was destroyed, the Jewish Christians were a minority among the total number of Christians, and it was becoming clear that the future of the new religion would be dominated by Gentile Christians. Nevertheless, the tannaim came into contact primarily with Jewish Christians and so continued to regard the Christians as Jews who had gone astray by following the teachings of Jesus.

The Benediction against the Minim

A new set of circumstances confronted the tannaitic leadership when it reassembled at Yavneh after the war with Rome was lost. By this time, the need to close ranks and to face the future as a united community was greater than ever. We shall see, though, that the Rabbis still did not elect to see the Jewish Christians as a separate religion. After all, they still met the halakhic criteria for Jewish status. Instead, action would be taken to bar them from officiating as precentors in the synagogue in order to make them feel unwanted there and to exclude their books from sanctified status. Other restrictions would attempt to separate the Jewish Christians from

the mainstream Jewish community. Tannaitic law would eventually
have to face the Gentile Christians, but the Rabbis as yet had little
opportunity for contact with them.

While our sources show no attempt on the part of the tannaim to
read anyone out of the Jewish people on account of heretical beliefs,
the Rabbis did impose certain restrictions on those whom they
regarded as standing outside the accepted system of Jewish belief.
Such heretics who were subjected to legal restrictions are termed
minim.

While this term itself has constituted a major scholarly problem,
it is now agreed that it was a general term for heretics, applied at
various times in the Rabbinic period to different groups which
presented doctrinal challenges to Rabbinic Judaism while remain-
ing, from a halakhic point of view, within the fold.[8] A number of
tannaitic restrictions directed against *minim* clearly refer to the early
Jewish Christians, as can be shown from their content and date.[9]
These regulations show how the Rabbis attempted to combat those
beliefs which they regarded as outside the Jewish pale while never
rejecting the Jewishness of those who held them.

The primary area in which the tannaim imposed restrictions on
the Jewish Christians was in regard to the synagogue. The *birkat
ha-minim,* the benediction against heretics, was adapted from an
older benediction, the purpose of which was to ask divine punishment on the *paroshim,* those who had separated themselves from the
community. This benediction was now reformulated to include
explicit mention of the *minim,* here primarily Jewish Christians. In
this way, the *birkat ha-minim* functioned to exclude such people from
serving as precentors in the synagogue.[10] Indeed, this benediction
probably went a long way toward making the Jewish Christians feel
unwelcome in the synagogue and causing them to worship separately.

A *baraita'* in B. Berakhot 28bf. states:[11]

Our Rabbis taught: Simeon Ha-Paqoli ordered[12] the Eighteen
Benedictions[13] before Rabban Gamliel at Yavneh.[14] Rabban Gamliel

said to the Sages: Is there no one who knows how to compose a benediction against the *minim?*[15] Samuel Ha-Qaṭan stood up[16] and composed it. Another year (while serving as precentor), he (Samuel Ha-Qaṭan) forgot it[17] and tried to recall it[18] for two or three hours,[19] yet they did not remove him.[20]

Despite some ingenious claims to the contrary,[21] the Gamliel of our *baraita'* is Rabban Gamliel II of Yavneh in the post-destruction period.[22] Simeon Ha-Paqoli set the Eighteen Benedictions in order before Rabban Gamliel as part of the general effort at Yavneh to fix and standardize *halakhah.* Rabban Gamliel (II) asked for a volunteer to compose the benediction against the *minim.* Samuel Ha-Qaṭan stood up and adapted the previously existing benediction to include the *minim.*[23] In a later year, he was called upon to serve as precentor. In the course of the service, he was unable to recite the benediction against the *minim.* Nonetheless, even after several hours of trying to recall it, the Rabbis did not remove him as precentor.

B. Berakhot 29a asks why he was not removed. After all, it was the purpose of this blessing to ensure that the precentor was not one of those heretics cursed in the benediction.[24] The Talmud answers that since Samuel Ha-Qaṭan had himself composed it, it could be assumed that he was not a *min.*

Since the term *min* can refer at different times to various forms of heresy that threatened Rabbinic Judaism in Talmudic times, it is essential to clarify who the *minim* of this benediction are. Palestinian texts of the Eighteen Benedictions from the Cairo Genizah present us with a text of the benediction which elucidates the identification of the *minim:*[25]

> For the apostates may there be no hope unless they return to Your Torah. As for the *noṣerim* and the *minim,* may they perish immediately. Speedily may they be erased from the Book of Life and may they not be registered among the righteous. Blessed are You, O Lord, Who subdues the wicked.

While other specimens of the Palestinian liturgy show slight variation, the *noṣerim,* (usually translated "Christians") and *minim* are included in the best texts of this benediction.[26] Some may wish to debate whether the *noṣerim* and *minim* here mentioned are to be taken as one group or two. Yet the fact remains that the *noṣerim* were included with apostates and heretics in the Genizah documents.

May we assume that this version of the benediction represents the text as it was recited by Samuel Ha-Qaṭan before the sages of Yavneh? On the one hand, the Palestinian liturgical material found in the Cairo Genizah generally preserves the traditions of Palestinian Jewry in the amoraic period. On the other hand, there may be external evidence that this benediction was recited during the tannaitic period and that it included explicit reference to *noṣerim.*

Three passages in the Gospel of John (9:22, 12:42, 16:2) mention the expulsion of Christians from the synagogue. The Gospel of John was most probably not composed until at least the last decade of the first century. The actual setting of the Gospel is not known, although some would place it in a Syrian or Palestinian milieu.[27] The most we can conclude from John is that the community to which it was directed *may* have already been subject to the benediction against the *minim* when this book was composed.[28]

Justin Martyr, writing in the middle of the second century C.E., in his Dialogue with Tryphon[29] referred several times to the cursing of Christians in the synagogue. Justin castigates his interlocutor Trypho as follows (XVI):[30]

> For you slew the just one (Jesus) and his prophets before him, and now you . . . dishonour those that set their hope on him, and God Almighty and Maker of the Universe that sent him, cursing in your synagogues them that believe in Christ.

In XLVII, he writes:[31]

> I declare that they of the seed of Abraham who live according to the Law . . . will not be saved, and especially they who in the synagogues have anathematized, and still anathematize, those who believe in that very Christ. . . .

In XCIII, Justin accuses the Jews first of the murder of Jesus and then of [32]

> cursing even them who prove that he who was crucified by you is the Christ.

In CVIII, Justin accuses the Jews of cursing both Jesus and those who believe in him.[33] Finally he appeals to the Jews in CXXXVII not to revile Jesus:[34]

> As the rulers of your synagogues teach you, after the prayer.

It is difficult to escape the conclusion that these passages are a polemical and confused reflection of the recitation of the *birkat ha-minim* in the synagogues of Palestine (Justin grew up in Samaria). These passages present evidence that some version of the benediction was already recited in the mid-second century c.e. and that it included explicit reference to the Christians.

Similar testimony comes from Origen (c. 185–c. 254 c.e.), who accuses Jews of blaspheming and cursing Jesus[35] and in another passage says:[36]

> Enter the synagogue of the Jews and see Jesus flagellated by those with the language of blasphemy.

It has been rightly observed, however, that this passage makes no explicit mention of the cursing of the Christians or of the role of such cursing in Jewish liturgy.[37]

Explicit reference, however, comes from Epiphanius and Jerome. Epiphanius (c. 315–403 c.e.), speaking of the Nazoraeans, a Judaizing Christian sect, says:[38]

> . . . the people also stand up in the morning, at noon, and in the evening, three times a day and they pronounce curses and maledictions over them when they say their prayers in the synagogues. Three times a day they say: "May God curse the Nazoraeans."

Whereas Epiphanius took the prayer in question to refer to members of the Judaizing Christian sect of the Nazoraeans,[39] Jerome (342–420 C.E.) understood it to refer to Christians in general (called Nazarenes). Jerome states:[40]

> . . . until today in their synagogues they [the Jews] blaspheme the Christian people under the name Nazarenes.

In another passage he says:[41]

> . . . up to the present day they [the Jews] persevere in blasphemy and three times a day in all the synagogues they anathematize the Christian name under the name of Nazarenes.

Elsewhere, speaking of Jesus, Jerome writes:[42]

> . . . for they [the Jews] curse him in their synagogues three times every day under the name of Nazarenes.

and finally:[43]

> . . . in your synagogues, who night and day blaspheme the Saviour, they utter curses against the Christians three times a day, as I have said, under the name of Nazarenes.

R. Kimelman has recently maintained that Epiphanius correctly interpreted the text of the benediction as referring to the Nazoraean sect, but that Jerome took it as referring to Christians in general.[44] In fact, it is certain that Epiphanius erred. Careful examination of the Latin text of Jerome indicates that he distinguished between the Nazarenes, Christians in general, and the Nazoraeans, the Judaizing Christians of whom he speaks at length.[45] In fact, the malediction delivered in the synagogue is said by him to refer to the Nazarenes or Christians. It was Epiphanius or his source that confused the two terms and mistook the Hebrew *noṣerim* as a reference to the Nazoraean sect of his day.

In seeking to claim that Jerome is actually referring to a curse of the Nazoraeans, Kimelman quotes a passage from Jerome. The passage, properly understood, however, indicates that to Jerome the Christians were cursed along with the *minim* in the synagogues of his time. The passage is as follows:[46]

> Until now a heresy is to be found in all parts of the East where Jews have their synagogues; it is called "of the Minaeans (*Minaeorum*)" and cursed by the Pharisees up to now. Usually they are called Nazoraeans (*Nazaraeos*). They believe in Christ, son of God, born of Mary the Virgin, and they say about him that he suffered and rose again under Pontius Pilate, which we also believe, but since they want to be both Jews and Christians, they are neither Jews nor Christians.

Now this passage explicitly states that "Nazoraeans" are the usual designation for the group which the Jews have called *minim*. In other words, the term *minim*, already found in the Yavnean version of the *birkat ha-minim*, was taken by Jerome to refer to the Nazoraeans of his day. The designation "Nazarenes," whom Jerome elsewhere says were also cursed in this benediction, must therefore have referred to the Gentile Christians. We must conclude that there indeed was a benediction against Christians in general in the time of Jerome and Epiphanius, and Jerome bears certain witness to it.

To further buttress his argument, Kimelman maintains that Hebrew *noṣerim*, which he vocalizes *naṣrim*, likewise refers to the Nazoraeans, rather than to the Nazarenes.[47] This is extremely doubtful. Throughout uncensored Rabbinic texts the term *noṣri* appears as a description of Jesus.[48] Without attempting to determine here whether this word is to be derived from the place-name Nazareth or from the Hebrew verb *nṣr*, "to watch, guard," it will be noted that *noṣri* came into prominence in Hebrew as a description of early Christianity. To the Rabbis, this term continued to describe the ever-changing Christian community in Palestine, so that in amoraic texts it refers to Christians in general.[49] By this time, the vast majority of Christians were Gentile, and it is to them that this term must have referred. It is extremely forced to maintain that the term

in Rabbinic texts could refer to the Nazoraeans, a group for which
we have evidence of neither Rabbinic contact nor knowledge.
Indeed, the Nazoraean sect was a curiosity even to the church
fathers. It may have always been numerically insignificant, especially
if we judge from comparison with accounts of the Ebionites to
whom much greater prominence is given.[50]

Hebrew *noṣerim,* as reflected in the Nazarenes of Jerome, can only
refer to Christians in general. It cannot be maintained that it refers
to the sect of the Nazoraeans. Hence, it is certain that in the fourth
century the benediction against the *minim* included explicit mention
of the Christians.

This curse could only be found in the Eighteen Benedictions
since it would be the only thrice-daily recitation in the synagogue
services. If Justin Martyr was referring to this benediction, then we
would have confirmation from the mid-second century that the
Christians were specifically mentioned in this prayer. Further, while
the version before us differentiates *minim* from Christians, it should
be remembered that many Rabbinic texts speak of the *minim* and
clearly designate believers in Jesus. It is most likely, however, that
our benediction meant to distinguish Jewish Christians from Gentile
Christians and that the *minim* were Jewish Christians while the
noṣerim (like the Nazarenes) were Gentile Christians.

If this last interpretation is correct, it is possible to trace the
development of this benediction. The original threat to Judaism was
from Jewish Christianity, and so a reference against the *minim* (a
general term here referring to Jewish Christians) was introduced
into a previously existing benediction. At some later date, perhaps
by 150 C.E. but definitely by 350 C.E., as the fate of Christianity as a
Gentile religion was sealed, the mention of Gentile Christians was
added to the prayer as well.

The specific effect of the benediction was to insure that those
who were *minim* would not serve as precentors in the synagogue.
After all, no one would be willing to pray for his own destruction. It
was assumed that the institution of such a benediction would lead

ultimately to the exclusion of the *minim* from the synagogue. Such a benediction in its original form can have been directed only against Jews who despite their heretical beliefs were likely to be found in the synagogue. Gentile Christians would not have been in the synagogue nor would they have been called upon to serve as precentors. When the separation of the Jewish Christians from the synagogue was accomplished, the prayer was retained as a general malediction and prayer for the destruction of the enemies of Israel. Therefore, the *noṣerim* were also added.

That such a development actually took place in the benediction is clear from the church fathers.[51] Only in Epiphanius (c. 315–403 C.E.) and Jerome (342–420 C.E.) do we find explicit reference to the *noṣerim* in the *birkat ha-minim*. This is because the *noṣerim* were added to the benediction after the time of Justin and Origen, whose allusions to the benediction make no mention of this specific term. By the time of Epiphanius and Jerome, the Roman Empire, now Christian, had imposed various anti-Jewish measures. It was only natural to add explicit mention of the Gentile Christians to this prayer.

It cannot be overemphasized that while the benediction against the *minim* sought to exclude Jewish Christians from active participation in the synagogue service, it in no way implied expulsion from the Jewish people. In fact, heresy, no matter how great, was never seen as cutting the heretic's tie to Judaism. Not even outright apostasy could overpower the halakhic criteria for Jewish identification which were outlined above.[52] When the method of excommunication was used to separate heretics from the Jewish community in the Middle Ages,[53] even this measure, which was to a great extent a medieval halakhic development, did not in any way cancel the Jewish status of the excommunicant. Indeed, regardless of the transgressions of a Jew, he was a Jew under any and all circumstances, even though his rights within *halakhah* might be limited as a result of his actions.

Opposition to Christian Scriptures

While the benediction against the *minim* was certainly the most important step taken by the tannaim to combat Jewish Christianity, they also took steps to emphasize that the Christian Scriptures were not holy.[54] First, the Jewish Christians themselves wrote scrolls of the Bible (*sifre minim*). The question here was the sanctity of the entire text. Second, beginning in the second half of the first century, early recensions of the Gospels and Epistles began to circulate. The sanctity of those sections of these Christian texts which quoted the Hebrew Scriptures directly also had to be determined. In view of the role of the Gospels and Epistles as a vehicle for the dissemination of Christianity, it is easy to understand why the Rabbis went out of their way to divest them of sanctity and halakhic status.

T. Shabbat 13(14):5 deals with these texts:[55]

> We do not save from a fire[56] (on the Sabbath) the Gospels[57] and the books of the *minim* ("heretics"). Rather, they are burned in their place, they and their Tetragrammata. Rabbi Yose Ha-Gelili says: During the week, one should cut out their Tetragrammata and hide them away and burn the remainder. Said Rabbi Ṭarfon: May I bury my sons![58] If (these books) would come into my hand, I would burn them[59] along with their Tetragrammata. For even if a pursuer[60] were running after me, I would enter a house[61] of idolatry rather than enter their (the Jewish Christians') houses. For the idolators do not know Him and deny Him,[62] but these (Jewish Christians) know Him and deny Him. . . . Said Rabbi Ishmael: If in order to bring[63] peace between a husband and his wife, the Everpresent has commanded[64] that a book[65] which has been written in holiness be erased by means of water, how much more so should the books of the *minim* which bring enmity[66] between Israel and their Father Who is in Heaven be erased,[67] they and their Tetragrammata. . . . Just as we do not save them from a fire, so we do not save them from a cave-in[68] nor from[69] water nor from anything which would destroy them.

The passage contains no disagreement regarding what to do if the Gospels or other books of the *minim* (texts of the Hebrew Scriptures)[70] are caught in a fire on the Sabbath. These books are not to be saved, as they have no sanctity. There is, however, debate regarding what to do with such texts during the week. Rabbi Yose Ha-Gelili suggests removing the Tetragrammata and burning the rest. Apparently, he feels that regardless of who wrote it, the Tetragrammaton retains its sanctity. Rabbi Ṭarfon permits the burning of the texts with their divine names. Rabbi Ishmael agrees with Rabbi Ṭarfon and supports his view with an analogy to the bitter waters of the suspected adulteress. Further, Rabbi Ṭarfon regards these Jewish Christians as worse than idolators, for while it was understandable that a pagan might embrace the new faith, it was a great source of frustration that Jews, raised in the traditions of Judaism, would do so as well.[71]

In regard to dating, the named authorities in the debate are all Yavneans who flourished in the period leading up to the Bar Kokhba Revolt. We see that the Jewish Christians were using Hebrew texts of the Bible, and that there were early recensions of the Gospels already in circulation. A decision, therefore, had to be rendered regarding the halakhic status of these texts. This Tosefta passage is indicative of the emerging view of the tannaim. By this time, more and more Gentiles had joined the Church, and the Scriptures of the Christians had begun to be read in Palestine. The Rabbis had to take a stand indicating the heretical nature of these texts in the early years of the second century.

Further reference to the very same texts appears in T. Yadayim 2:13:[72]

> The Gospels and the books of the *minim* ("heretics") do not defile the hands. . . .

The "defilement of the hands" was a sign of canonicity in tannaitic texts.[73] Books of the Bible which defiled the hands were Holy Scriptures. In spite of the appearance of verses from the Hebrew Bible in the Gospels, this passage indicates that they, and even texts of the Hebrew Bible written by *minim*, have absolutely no sanctity.

While there is no indication of date in this passage, it seems that it would emerge from the same period as the previous text. Indeed, in the years before the Bar Kokhba Revolt, there was a need to accent the illegitimacy of Jewish Christianity. The two passages we have studied here indicate clearly that the transgressions of the *minim* were sufficient to render their texts of the Hebrew Bible unholy. The tannaim sought in this way to clearly differentiate Christianity from Judaism, but they did not attempt to disavow the Jewishness of the *minim* at any time.

Prohibition on Contact with the Minim

T. Hullin 2 contains a series of traditions regarding *minim*, which in the opinion of the redactor referred to the Jewish Christians. Even if these traditions were actually applied to all kinds of *minim*, they portray something of the tannaitic attitude to the Jewish Christians evident in halakhic enactments. Below, we will take up the two stories (*ma'asim*) which appear immediately after these legal traditions.

T. Hullin 2:20–21 states:[74]

> If meat is found in the hand of a non-Jew, it is permitted to derive benefit from it. (If it is found) in the hand of a *min*, it is forbidden to derive benefit from it. That which comes forth from the house of a *min*,[75] indeed it is the meat of sacrifices to the dead (idolatrous worship),[76] for they said: The slaughtering of a *min* is idolatry; their bread is the bread of a Samaritan; their wine is the wine of (idolatrous) libation; their fruits are untithed; their books are the books of diviners,[77] and their children are *mamzerim*. We do not sell to them, nor do we buy from them. We do not take from them, nor do we give to them,[78] and we do not teach their sons a craft. We are not healed by them, neither healing of property nor healing of life.[79]

First, it must be determined whether this text refers to Jewish Christians or to other *minim*. From some amoraic texts we gain the impression that the Rabbis accused the early Christians of sexual immorality.[80] It is difficult to determine if this claim was engendered by the communal life practiced in the early church or if it stemmed from the attitude of the Rabbis toward the status of Jesus[81] in light of the Christian traditions regarding his birth. Our passage, in stating that the children of *minim* are *mamzerim,* the offspring of illegal unions, is, in fact, accusing the *minim* of sexual immorality. Such a claim may be easily understood in light of the Rabbinic accusation if the *minim* in question are early Jewish Christians.

The accusation that the books of the *minim* are magical books is most appropriate if the *minim* in question are Jewish Christians, since we know that the early Rabbinic tradition saw Jesus as a magical practitioner above all.[82] Further, only in reference to the Jewish Christians do we find a parallel to the accusation that their books were not sacred. We have seen in two texts discussed above[83] that even their copies of the Bible were considered devoid of sanctity. Internal evidence in this text, then, seems to show that it refers to Jewish Christians. The two stories which follow our passage in T. Hullin 2:22–24 deal explicitly with cases of *minim* who were Jewish Christians. Clearly, then, the redactor, who grouped these traditions in the midst of a chapter dealing with the requirements of ritual slaughter, was of the opinion that the *minim* in our halakhic text were Jewish Christians. We must emphasize that even if *minim* here is a general term, the prescriptions of those *halakhot* would still have been applied by the tannaim to the early Jewish Christians.

As the tradition stands, it is redacted of two parts. First comes a statement of *halakhah* regarding meat in the hands of a non-Jew and that of a *min.* The formulator of this *halakhah,* in order to prove his point, appeals to an even earlier tannaitic statement regarding the *minim* which in itself contains the same ruling regarding the meat of a *min.*[84] Then comes a second *halakhah* forbidding various kinds of commercial and social contact with *minim.* In other words, there are at least two stages in the history of the tradition before us. As to the dating, little can be said with certainty from this passage alone except that it was probably formulated before the Bar Kokhba

Revolt. A text to be studied in the next section will suggest a *terminus ante quem* of the end of the first century C.E.[85]

We shall have to analyze the statements separately as regards their content. The opening clause concerns only meat and is appropriate to this tractate which deals with the laws of ritual slaughter of meat outside the Temple precincts. The law presumes that meat found in the possession of a non-Jew may have been slaughtered by him. Although forbidden to be eaten, such meat may be sold or benefit may be otherwise derived from it. It is, however, forbidden even to derive benefit from meat in the hands of a *min*. The reason for this stringent ruling is given. The meat, presumed to have been slaughtered by a *min,* is considered to be of the status of that slaughtered by an idolator. Meat presumed slaughtered by an idolator is not only forbidden to be eaten, but it is also forbidden to sell it or to otherwise derive benefit from it.

In the second part of our tradition, beginning "for they said" (*mi-pene she-'ameru*), an entire list of restrictions regarding the status of the *min* in Rabbinic law is mentioned. This list is formulated in polemical tone and certainly comes from a period in which greater animus was directed to the issue at hand. We find that not only is it in regard to meat that he is treated like an idolator. His bread is considered "Samaritan bread"[86] and hence it is forbidden to be eaten or to derive benefit from it. Likewise, his wine is not only forbidden as would be that of any non-Jew, but it is also prohibited to derive any benefit from it, as is the case with wine used for idolatrous libations. Fruits which are in the hands of a *min* are considered to be untithed, so that a pious Jew may not eat them, for their priestly and Levitical portions have not been separated.

After these dietary restrictions come the two matters referred to already. Their books are considered not to be holy, as we have already seen from our extensive discussion of the status of the Scriptures of the Jewish Christians above. Their children are considered the offspring of prohibited marriages. Finally, there is a separate *halakhah* including further prohibitions. All business dealings with them are prohibited. It is forbidden to teach their children a craft, or to make use of their medical skills, a matter to which we will return in the next section.[87]

It will be instructive to examine the social context of these laws. We are clearly dealing with restrictions which are aimed at members of the Jewish community. In order to attempt to isolate these people, a series of restrictions places them on a par with idolators. Yet even so, the Jewish status of the *min* remains unquestionable. His children are to be considered *mamzerim*. The status of *mamzer* has no relevance in *halakhah* in reference to non-Jews. It is a status which can apply only to Jews and which, therefore, shows once again that the Jewish Christians who are referred to in our text are considered Jews. Our study of this complex of *halakhot* has again shown that the Jewish status of a person is not surrendered, regardless of his transgressions, and certainly not as a result of heretical beliefs.

Apparently, then, the tannaim still regarded the Jewish Christians they knew as Jews, even as late as the end of the first century C.E. Although by this time Gentile Christians constituted a majority of the believers in the new religion, the impact of this situation had not yet been felt in Palestine where Jewish Christianity still predominated until the Bar Kokhba Revolt.

VI.   The Jewish Christians in Tannaitic Narrative

Alongside the references to Jewish Christians in the tannaitic period which we have studied so far, there are also two tannaitic narratives (ma'asim) worthy of consideration. It is only from the halakhic passages we have already studied that we can understand how the tannaim took action against Christianity while still taking for granted the Jewish status of the Jewish Christians. Nevertheless, it is instructive to see how the tensions we have been studying are reflected in the narratives.

Both of the stories to be considered here are included in the very same chapter in T. Hullin in which the halakhic passage just studied is found. The three passages form a unit, placed within the context of the laws of ritual slaughter. The redactor apparently found before him a halakhic passage dealing with the meat of a *min* (which itself was a composite, as mentioned above) which had already been combined with the two narrative traditions regarding *minim*. He placed these together, as he had received them, in the Tosefta.[1] If we examine the entire group of passages together, we see that the first story (T. Hullin 2:22–23) is meant to illustrate the prohibition of medical treatment by a *min*. The second story (T. Hullin 2:24) intends to illustrate that it is forbidden to derive even the slightest benefit from a *min*, a principle which underlies the detailed prescriptions of the second part (from "for they said") in the halakhic passages we have just examined (T. Hullin 2:20–21).

Rabbi Eleazar ben Damah and the Jewish Christian Healer

Now that the context has been established, we may turn to the first narrative, T. Hullin 2:22–23:[2]

69

It happened that a snake bit Rabbi Eleazar ben Damah.[3] Jacob of Kefar Sama[4] came to heal him in the name of Yeshua ben Pantira (Jesus),[5] but Rabbi Ishmael did not allow him. He (Rabbi Ishmael)[6] said to him (Rabbi Eleazar ben Damah), "You are not permitted, Ben Damah." He (Rabbi Eleazar ben Damah) said to him (Rabbi Ishmael), "I will bring you a proof that he may heal me."[7] He did not have time to bring the proof before he died. Said Rabbi Ishmael, "Fortunate are you, Ben Damah, for you departed in peace[8] and you did not break through the fence[9] of the sages. For anyone who breaks through a fence of the sages, at the end misfortune will come upon him, as it is said (Eccl. 10:8): 'And as to one who breaks[10] a fence, a snake shall bite him.'"

This passage provides us with a *terminus ante quem* for the halakhic ruling that one may not be healed by a *min*. Indeed, the ruling had to be in existence before the dispute between Rabbi Ishmael and the dying Rabbi Eleazar ben Damah. R. T. Herford has argued that the event behind this narrative must have taken place before 130 C.E., sometime during the Ushan period.[11] In other words, the ruling in question is from the period in which the *minim* whom the Rabbis confronted were indeed the Jewish Christians. Further, it is from the period in which the Rabbis were intensifying their prohibitions on contact with Jewish Christians in an effort to stem the rising tide of Christianity.

The passage is also interesting for the social reality it paints. Jews and Jewish Christians are still in close contact, apparently in the villages of the Galilee. Jacob of Kefar Sama was apparently one of these Jewish Christians and must have been known as a healer or physician. There is no reason to believe that he is to be identified with the Jacob of Kefar Sikhnin whom we will meet in the next story. Jacob was a common name and must have been so as well among the early Jewish Christians.

Even some tannaim are not in agreement with this restriction and are willing to make use of cures even if they are to be accompanied by the mention of the name of Jesus in some form. Here we see the tensions among the tannaim about how far to go in their effort to make fences around the Torah and thus to separate the Jewish Christians from the mainstream of the Jewish community in the Land of Israel.

Rabbi Eliezer and the Accusation of Minut

The second of the two narratives is T. Ḥullin 2:24:[12]

It happened that Rabbi Eliezer was arrested on charges[13] of *minut*,[14] and they brought him up to the platform[15] to be tried. The governor[16] said to him, "Does an elder like yourself busy himself with things like these?" He (Rabbi Eliezer) said to him (the governor), "The judge is reliable[17] concerning me." The governor thought that he was referring to him, but he intended to refer to his Father Who is in heaven. He (the governor) said to him (Rabbi Eliezer), "Since you have accepted me as reliable concerning yourself, thus I have said: It is possible that these gray hairs[18] are in error concerning these charges.[19] *Dimissus*.[20] You are released." After he (Rabbi Eliezer) left the platform, he was troubled that he had been arrested on charges of *minut*. His disciples came in to console him, but he would not take (consolation). Rabbi Akiva entered and said to him, "My teacher, may I say before you something so that perhaps you will not grieve?" He said to him, "Say (it)." He (Rabbi Akiva) said to him (Rabbi Eliezer), "Perhaps one of the *minim* said a word of *minut* which gave you pleasure (*we-hina'akha*)?" He (Rabbi Eliezer) said, "By Heaven, you have reminded me. Once I was walking in the street[21] of Sepphoris. I chanced upon Jacob of Kefar Sikhnin, and he said a word of *minut* in the name of Yeshua ben Panṭira (Jesus), and it gave me pleasure (*we-hin'ani*). I was arrested on charges of *minut*, for I transgressed the words of the Torah,[22] 'Keep your path far from her and do not draw near to the entrance of her house (Prov. 5:8), for she has brought down many victims [and numerous are those whom she has killed] (Prov. 7:26).'" For Rabbi Eliezer used to say: "Stay away from ugliness and from that which resembles ugliness."

The main body of the passage before us is in three parts. First comes the story of how Rabbi Eliezer outwitted the governor. Then we have the scene with his students which serves as a transition to the account of his meeting with Jacob of Kefar Sikhnin.[23] To this collection a statement which is widespread in Rabbinic literature regarding avoidance of ugliness is appended, probably by a later transmitter of these traditions. After all, the transition here is not smooth ("for," Hebrew *she-*). The statement is here attributed to Rabbi Eliezer, although elsewhere it is not.[24] The teacher who attached this last passage to the *ma'aseh* did so to explain Rabbi Eliezer's reference to the passage in Proverbs more clearly. We will be concerned here only with the story itself.

Rabbi Eliezer is arrested for *minut*. From the continuation of the story it is certain that he was accused of Jewish Christianity during the rule of Trajan[25] by the Roman authorities who were at the time persecuting Jewish Christians. Indeed, this event must have occurred in 109 C.E. at the same time as the crucifixion of the Bishop of Jerusalem reported by Eusebius.[26]

An examination of the legal details of the story leads to the conclusion that the setting of the trial as it appears here is historical.[27] On the other hand, the attempt to demonstrate Rabbi Eliezer's cleverness is characteristic of the kind of story that might be created in later periods. We cannot be certain, therefore, that the narrative demonstrates a Rabbinic encounter with Jewish Christianity in the time of Rabbi Eliezer. It may reflect a somewhat later reality instead. The second section is clearly meant to demonstrate the wisdom of Rabbi Akiva.[28]

Interesting is the amazement of the Roman governor. Faced with a Rabbi, he is amazed to find that he is an adherent of Jewish Christianity.[29] When the Rabbi cleverly states his *double entendre*, he leaves the governor with the impression that he is accepting the testimony of the judge himself as reliable in his case, while really intending to accept God's justness. The governor himself has already testified that it is unlikely that a Rabbi would be a Christian and so proclaims him free and dismisses the case.

At the same time, we should note the attestations from this and later periods of the presence of *minim* at Sepphoris.[30] The exchange with the Jewish Christian Jacob of Kefar Sikhnin, describing him as it does by name, also has the ring of historicity. It seems to us then to be probable, although not certain, that the events described in our account did occur. Already in 109 A.D. the tanna Rabbi Eliezer ben Hyrcanus was in contact with Jewish Christians in Sepphoris. He blamed his arrest on his failure to follow the advice of Proverbs to keep clear of their influence.

In context in T. Hullin 2, this passage comes as an addition to the prohibition of deriving benefit (*hana'ah*) of any kind from Jewish Christians (*minim*).[31] Rabbi Eliezer ben Hyrcanus allowed himself to receive pleasure (benefit) (*we-hina'akha . . . we-hin'ani . . .*) from the words of a Jewish Christian and even this, in his own view and that of Rabbi Akiva, led him to receive recompense and to be arrested and narrowly escape prosecution as a Jewish Christian. Certainly, the lesson is that even the most minimal contact with the *minim* can ultimately lead one down their path.[32]

Secondary, expanded versions of this story appear in amoraic sources.[33] These accounts supply the words of Jacob of Kefar Sikhnin, the Jewish Christian. These are said to relate to the exegesis of Deut. 23:18 in light of Micah 1:7. It is certain that these expanded versions are secondary. At the same time, they represent a tradition which presumed the discussion between Rabbi Eliezer ben Hyrcanus and the Jewish Christian to have related to issues of scriptural exegesis. After all, this was indeed the major issue to be debated by Jews and Jewish Christians in the years leading up to the Bar Kokhba Revolt. Both communities accepted the same Scriptures as canonical. They disagreed, however, on how those Scriptures were to be interpreted. Thus far, at every stage we have examined, the Rabbis continued to relate to the Jewish Christians as Jews who went astray but whose identity as Jews was unquestionable. We shall now have to ask what caused the Rabbis to alter that conception, and what led the tannaim to conclude that the Christians were to be regarded as a separate religious community.

VII.   Conclusion: The Final Break

For the Jewish community of Palestine, the years between 80 and 130 C.E. were simultaneously years of reconstruction of the country and preparation for the Bar Kokhba Revolt. Throughout this period Christianity continued to grow while its Jewish element was being reduced. In actual fact the juridical basis for the Gentile domination of Christianity was laid in the time of Paul, when the legitimacy of Gentile Christianity was established.[1] The effect of these actions was not actually felt by the tannaim until the early years of the second century.

By the time of the Bar Kokhba war (132–35 C.E.), Gentile Christianity had most probably still not taken over the Jerusalem Church nor become the dominant element in the Palestinian Christian community. Accordingly, the tannaim would still have seen the early Christians as Jews.

The Bar Kokhba Revolt did much, however, to highlight the emerging separation of the Christians from the Jewish community. It is certain that among the factors contributing to both the popular and Rabbinic support enjoyed by Bar Kokhba was the view of some who saw Bar Kokhba as a Messianic figure.[2] Indeed, some of the leaders of the earlier revolt against Rome (66–74 C.E.) had also been seen in the same light.[3] For this reason, Jewish Christians did not support Bar Kokhba and refused to participate in the rebellion. After all, Jesus was their savior, so they could not fight on behalf of another Messiah.[4] Furthermore, they probably took the view later expressed by the church fathers that the destruction of Jerusalem and Judea in the Great Revolt of 66–74 C.E. was a just punishment for the Jewish rejection of the Messiahship of Jesus. According to later accounts preserved in the church fathers, the refusal to support his revolt may even have led Bar Kokhba to attack Jewish Christians.[5] Subsequently, the general dislocation brought about by the war and other factors—some of which are still not clear—led to a large decrease in the number of Jewish Christians in Palestine, and this at a time when the number of Gentile Christians in the Roman world, and even in Palestine itself, was increasing rapidly.

But the Romans themselves helped to bring about the final break. When the city of Jerusalem was turned into Aelia Capitolina in the aftermath of the Bar Kokhba war, Jews, including Jewish Christians, were prohibited from entering the city.[6] Therefore, the Jerusalem Church was henceforth to be an essentially Gentile one, led by a Gentile bishop. The Roman prohibition of circumcision, probably promulgated before the war but enforced immediately afterwards,[7] must have discouraged conversion to Jewish Christianity even further. The Jewish Christians, then, dissipated into small sectarian groups, most surviving in Trans-Jordan and Syria, so that after the Bar Kokhba war, Christianity, even in the Land of Israel, was no longer Jewish but Gentile.[8] The Rabbis ceased to deal with Jews who had gone astray but who still fulfilled the halakhic requirements of Jewish identity. They now confronted Gentiles who had converted to a religion which had rejected circumcision, the Jewish law of conversion, and the requirements of life under the *halakhah*. Only in this way had Christianity become a separate religion. It was now that the Rabbis dealt with Christians as members of a different and hostile religious community.[9]

The reports of the church fathers relative to what are usually called Jewish Christian sects[10] in the Bar Kokhba period indicate that these "Jewish Christians" had left or been expelled from the mainstream of Christianity. From our point of view, however, we must note the ambivalence of the sources on the actual Jewish status of these people. It would seem very likely that most of these sectarians were in reality *Judaizing* Christians who attempted to observe the Law as did the Jews without being of Jewish descent or Jews from the standpoint of the *halakhah*. The accusations by church fathers to the effect that these people were Jews[11] must be contrasted with those stating that they were neither Jews nor Christians.[12] The church fathers, in their zeal to uproot circumcision and the Law which required it, unleashed the accusation of Jewishness against these Judaizers. Even if, as they claim, some of these sectarians were descended from some of the original members of the Jerusalem Jewish Christian church,[13] those who joined them would not have done so in accord with the Rabbinic laws of proselytism, and their acceptance of the Torah would certainly not have qualified according to Rabbinic precepts.[14] These groups did persist in the amoraic period. Yet by the coming of Islam they were but a historical memory of what might have been the Christian Church had the Jewish Christians of Jerusalem carried the day against the Pauline urge for liberation from the Law.

In retrospect, the *halakhot* we have studied were what maintained the identity of the Jewish people. Had the rabbis relaxed these standards, accepting either the semi-proselytes or the earliest Gentile Christians into the Jewish people, Christians would quickly have become the majority within the expanded community of "Israel." Judaism as we know it would have ceased to exist even before reaching its codification in the Mishnah and the other great compilations of the tannaitic tradition. Christianity would have been the sole heir to the traditions of biblical antiquity, and observance of the commandments of the Torah would have disappeared within just a few centuries. In short, it was the *halakhah* and its definition of Jewish identity which saved the Jewish people and its heritage from extinction as a result of the newly emerging Christian ideology.

The ultimate parting of the ways for Judaism and Christianity took place when the adherents to Christianity no longer conformed to the halakhic definitions of a Jew. As these *Gentile* Christians, never converted to Judaism through the legal requirements we have discussed, became the dominant stream in the Christian communities which the Rabbis confronted, even in Palestine, the Rabbis ceased to regard the Christians as a group of Jews with heretical views and Christianity as a Jewish sect. Rather, the Rabbis began to regard the Christians as members of a separate religious community, and their teachings a perversion of the biblical tradition. From then on, Christians and Jews began a long history of interreligious strife which played so tragic a part in medieval and modern history.

Notes

I. Introduction: At the Crossroads

1. See my "Jewish Sectarianism in Second Temple Times," *Great Schisms in Jewish History*, ed. R. Jospe and S. Wagner (1981), 1–46.

2. For a recent review of the Samaritan issue, see F. Dexinger, "Limits of Tolerance in Judaism: The Samaritan Example," *Jewish and Christian Self-Definition* II, ed. E. P. Sanders (1981), pp. 88–114, 327–38. See also R. J. Coggins, *Samaritans and Jews* (1975).

3. See J. Goldstein, "Jewish Acceptance and Rejection of Hellenism," *Self-Definition* II, pp. 64–87, 318–26.

4. For the views of Philo of Alexandria, see S. Belkin, *Philo and the Oral Law* (1940), pp. 44–48. While the evidence is not entirely conclusive, there is no reason to believe that Philo's full-fledged proselyte was any different from that of the Palestinian sages of his time.

5. Much of the material pertaining to the Qumran sect has been collected in C. Rabin, *Qumran Studies* (1957), pp. 53–70.

6. See J. Neusner, *Method and Meaning in Ancient Judaism* (1979), pp. 192–5.

7. Cf. the conclusion reached from the Christian sources by M. Smith, "Early Christianity and Judaism," *Great Confrontations in Jewish History*, ed. S. Wagner and A. Breck (1977), pp. 47–9. Smith writes, p. 48, ". . . the dispute between the Pharisees and the followers of Jesus . . . did not primarily or principally concern the question whether or not Jesus was the Messiah. On the contrary, the matter in dispute was the Christians' nonobservance of the law."

II. The Jew by Birth

1. MS Kaufmann: וכל מי שאין לה לא עליו ולא על אחרים קידושים הוולד כמוה. ואי זה זה? זה ולד שפחה ונוכרית. Cf. J. Neusner, *A History of the Mishnaic Law of Women*, Part IV (1980), pp. 249f. Significant variants from manuscripts and early editions will be noted throughout this study, although no effort will be made to present a complete critical apparatus for each text cited. All punctuation and translation are mine. For a different perspective on this text, cf. D. Daube, "Conversion to Judaism and Earliest Christianity," *Ancient Jewish Law, Three Inaugural Lectures* (1981), pp. 22–32.

2. לא is omitted in MS Paris and in *ed. princ.*

3. Natronai Gaon (719–30 C.E.) explained that this refers to a bondwoman belonging to someone else. For if he married his own bondwoman, it would be assumed that he freed her and, therefore, the children would be Jewish. Other geonim, however, disagreed. See B. M. Lewin, *'Osar Ha-Ge'onim* VII (1936), to B. Yevamot 23a. This geonic controversy was not merely theoretical but involved the status of actual children.

4. The reading נכרית in *ed. princ.* (without the copulative *waw*) is clearly an error. Cf. M. Yevamot 2:5.

5. For a detailed discussion, see below, p. 11.

6. *Mevo'ot Le-Sifrut Ha-Tanna'im* (1957), pp. 414f.

7. *Massekhet 'Arayot We-Yuḥasin.*

8. For scriptural derivation, see B. Qiddushin 68a–b and P. Qiddushin 3:12 (ed. Krot. 3:14, 64d). Cf. also D. Halivni, *Meqorot U-Mesorot, Nashim* (1968) to B. Qiddushin 68a, pp. 703f.

9. MS Vienna, ed. S. Lieberman: גוי ועבד הבאו על בת ישראל והולידה בן, הולד ממזר. ר'
שמעון בן יהודה אומ' משם ר' שמעון: אין ממזר אלא מן האשה שאיסורה איסור ערוה וחייבין עליה כרת'.
Cf. Neusner, *Women* IV, pp. 256f.

10. MS Erfurt and *ed. princ.*: שבאו.

11. MS Erfurt: והולידו.

12. MS Erfurt: אלע', abbreviation for אלעזר.

13. MS Erfurt omits משם ר' שמעון.

14. Lev. 18:6–19, 20:11f., 14, 17, 19–21. Cf. Deut. 27:22f.

15. There is a great debate on the meaning of *karet* in the Bible. Cf. S. Loewenstamm, "Karet, Hikkaret," *'Enṣiqlopedyah Miqra'it* IV, 330–2. To the Rabbis it was either early death or childlessness. The mention of *karet* in this passage excludes two other groups of forbidden marriages: those imposed by the Rabbis (*sheniyyot*) and those mentioned in the Torah but for which execution by the court is prescribed. See Maimonides, H. 'Issure Bi'ah 1:18.

16. For the derivation of *mamzer,* see S. Loewenstamm, "Mamzer," *'Enṣiqlopedyah Miqra'it* V, 13. The *mamzer* is mentioned in Deut. 23:3.

17. M. Qiddushin 3:12, 4:1, T. Qiddushin 5:12.

18. For other sources taking the same view, see S. Lieberman, *TK,* ad loc. Note especially *Sifra' De-Ve Rav* (ed. Weiss), pp. 97c, 104c.

19. For Rabbi Simeon's view, see Lieberman, *TK,* ad loc. Cf. especially T. Yevamot 1:10 where the same view is expressed by Rabbi Eleazar (ben Shammua), a disciple of Rabbi Akiva who lived at about the time of the Bar Kokhba Revolt.

20. S. M. Passamaneck, "Some Medieval Problems in *Mamzeruth,*" *HUCA* 37 (1966), pp. 124, 126.

21. So D. Pardo, *Ḥasde David,* vol. I (1776), to T. Qiddushin 4:16. Cf. D.

Halivni, *Meqorot U-Mesorot, Nashim* to B. Yevamot 49a, and *Sifre Devarim* 248 (ed. Finkelstein, pp. 276f.).

22. Maimonides, *Perush Ha-Mishnayot,* ad loc. It is very likely that we are dealing with a case of historical development in this dispute. Originally, the *halakhah* considered the offspring of Gentile fathers and Jewish women to be *mamzerim.* Later on, it was ruled that they were not. Cf. also M. Bikkurim 1:45 according to which proselytes and their descendants do not read the first-fruits declaration, or say "our God and God of our fathers," or marry priests, "until their mother is a (full-fledged) Israelite." See also T. Bikkurim 1:2 for the opposing view of Rabbi Judah (and S. Lieberman, *TK,* ad loc. for the medieval commentators) and *Midrash Tanḥuma'* (ed. Buber), *Va-Yera',* p. 51a.

23. To the Rabbis there was no question that mixed marriages were forbidden. All halakhic rulings regarding the status of the children fall into the halakhic category of *be-di-'avad,* after the fact.

24. Ed. R. Marcus: ὡς παρὰ τὴν αὐτῶν δικαιοσύνην Ἡρώδῃ δώσουσι τὴν βασιλείαν ἰδιώτῃ τε ὄντι καὶ Ἰδουμαίῳ τουτέστιν ἡμιιουδαίῳ, δέον τοῖς ἐκ τοῦ γένους οὖσι παρέχειν ὡς ἔθος ἐστὶν αὐτοῖς. Our translation has been adapted from that of Marcus to accord with our interpretation of the passage.

25. This is the primary definition in Liddell and Scott.

26. So Marcus, and A. Schalit, *Yosef ben Matityahu (Flavius Yosefus), Qadmoniyyot Ha-Yehudim* III (1973), ad loc. Indeed, this definition is also attested in Liddell and Scott.

27. Ant. XIII, ix, 7 (257–8); Ant. XIV, i, 3 (8–9). Cf. E. Schürer, *A History of the Jewish People in the Age of Jesus Christ* I (1973), p. 234 n. 3, for contradictory reports. The report of Nicholaus of Damascus is properly debunked by Josephus. The views of the church fathers are to be explained as part of their negative view of Herod as slaughterer of the innocents (Math. 2:1–18).

28. Ant. XIV, vii, 3 (121); War I, viii, 9 (181).

29. Cf. my *"Giyyur Be-Khitve Yosef ben Matityahu, Izates Me-Ḥadayev Le-'Or Ha-Halakhah,"* *Yosef ben Matityahu, Historion shel 'Ereṣ Yisra'el,* ed. U. Rappaport (1982), p. 258 n. 40.

30. Deut. 17:15.

31. *Ed. princ.*: אגריפס המלך עמד וקבל, וקרא עמד, ושיבחוהו חכמים. ומשהגיע ״לא תוכל לתת עליך איש נכרי אשר לא אחיך הוא,״ זלגו דמעיו. אמרו לו: ״אל תיתירא אגריפס. אחינו אתה! אחינו אתה!״ Cf. Neusner, *Women* IV, p. 71.

32. The omission of עמד in MS Munich is a scribal error.

33. MSS Paris, Parma De Rossi 138, Parma "C" De Rossi 984, Munich, *ed. princ.*, and the unidentified edition published by Makor (Pisaro or Constantinople): ללא.

34. MSS Paris, Parma De Rossi 138, Munich, *ed. princ.*, and unidentified: זלגו

עיניו דמעות. MS Parma "C" De Rossi 984: וזלגו עיניו.

35. See Schürer I (1973), p. 447 n. 27.

36. Ant. XV, vii, 9 (255).

37. An alternative tendency in tannaitic tradition sees this entire episode negatively. Either because of illegitimacy of non-Davidic kingship, or because of the claim that Agrippa was in reality not Jewish according to *halakhah* (as Agrippa I was not), some tannaim expressed their doubts. A *baraita'* in B. Soṭah 41b in the name of Rabbi Nathan condemns the Jews for their flattering of Agrippa. P. Soṭah 7:7 (22a) quotes a *baraita'* in the name of Rabbi Haninah ben Gamliel which says that many Jews died on that day. Apparently, the version in *Sifre Devarim* 157 (ed. Finkelstein, p. 209) reflects this tendency. For this reason the words, "You are our brother!" attributed obliquely by the Mishnah to the sages (אמרו לו) are here attributed to *kol yisra'el*, "all of Israel." After all, how could the sages have sanctioned, let alone said, such words? Cf. the conflation of all these traditions in *Midrash Tanna'im* to Deut. 17:15 (ed. Hoffman I, p. 104). It is highly unlikely that the sages called Agrippa their brother only to comfort him. They must have meant it literally. Cf. Daube, pp. 23–25.

38. Or the grandchildren, so Rashi, ad loc.

39. Note that Ex. 34:15 singles out the threat of apostasy of Jewish girls through intermarriage, while Deut. 7:1–4 concentrates on the apostasy of sons.

40. *Toledot Ha-'Emunah Ha-Yisra'elit* (1966/7), IV, pp. 296–301.

41. For the Rabbis, Ruth was the archetype of the convert. See B. Bamberger, *Proselytism in the Talmudic Period* (1968), pp. 195–199. We do not mean to enter into the dispute regarding the date of the book of Ruth. We are speaking here of the story in the Bible in its historical setting.

42. C. Tchernowitz, *Toledot Ha-Halakhah* III (1953), p. 108, suggests that men could convert by circumcision but that no method was available for women.

43. This *midrash* is discussed in an unpublished section of my Brandeis University dissertation, *The Halakhah at Qumran* (1974), pp. 160–4.

44. See V. Aptowitzer, "*Spuren des Matriarchats im jüdischen Schrifttum (Schluss und Nachträge),*" *HUCA* 5 (1928), pp. 261–77.

45. The view of the Rabbis that the prohibition of Ammon and Moab applied only to males of these nations is certainly assumed in the book of Ruth. Otherwise, we should have expected the book to conceal the nationality of Ruth, especially in light of her being an ancestor of King David. Indeed, some modern scholars have seen the book as a polemical work seeking to prove that marriage to a Moabitess was permissible and that David was a legitimate king and dynast.

III.   Conversion to Judaism

1. We will return to the problem of God-fearers and semi-proselytes in the Hellenistic world. See below pp. 37f. For a survey of proselytism in Rabbinic

thought, see E. E. Urbach, *Ḥazal* (1971), pp. 480–94. On conversion, cf. Daube, pp. 1–22.

2. Ed. Horovitz (1966), p. 112: רבי אומר: מה ישראל שלא באו לברית אלא בשלשה דברים,
במילה ובטבילה ובהרצאית קרבן, אף הגרים כיוצא בהם. Cf. *Mekhilta' De-Rabbi Shim'on ben Yoḥai* to Ex. 12:48 (ed. Hoffmann [1905], p. 30), B. Keritot 9a and Gerim 2:4.

3. See the amoraic explanation in B. Keritot 9a (and *Tosafot*, ad loc.).

4. Ed Vilna: תנו רבנן: גר שבא להתגייר בזמן הזה, אומרים לו: מה ראית שבאת להתגייר? אי אתה יודע שישראל בזמן הזה דוים דחופים סחופים ומטורפין ויסורין באין עליהם? אם אומר יודע אני ואיני כדאי, מקבלין אותו מיד ומודיעין אותו מקצת מצות קלות ומקצת מצות חמורות, ומודיעין אותו עון לקט שכחה ופאה ומעשר עני. ומודיעין אותו ענשן של מצות. . . . וכשם שמודיעין אותו ענשן של מצות, כך מודיעין אותו מתן שכרן. . . . ואין מרבין עליו ואין מדקדקין עליו. קיבל, מלין אותו מיד. . . . נתרפא, מטבילין אותו מיד. ושני ת"ח עומדים על גביו ומודיעין אותו מקצת מצות קלות ומקצת מצות חמורות. טבל ועלה, הרי הוא כישראל לכל דבריו. אשה, נשים מושיבות אותה במים עד צוארה ושני ת"ח עומדים בחוץ ומודיעין אותה מקצת מצות קלות ומקצת מצות חמורות. . . . No differences of consequence are found in ed. Venice.

5. MS Munich omits בזמן הזה.

6. MS Munich omits שבאת.

7. MS Munich omits בזמן הזה but writes בזמן before שישראל. This is probably an error, the scribe's *Vorlage* containing a reading similar to that of the printed editions.

8. MS Munich reads ומסחפים and omits the copulative *waw* on the next word.

9. MS Vat. Ebr. 111 adds ומיד, probably under the influence of the continuation of the passage in which it occurs.

10. Cf. M. Avot 2:1, 4:2, and *Maḥazor Vitry* to Avot 2:1. Probably the terms lighter and heavier refer to the ease or difficulty of performance of the commandment.

11. For *'awon* as punishment for iniquity, see F. Brown, S. Driver, and C. Briggs, *A Hebrew and English Lexicon of the Old Testament*, p. 731.

12. Lev. 19:9, 23:22.

13. Deut. 24:19.

14. Lev. 19:9, 23:22.

15. Deut. 26:12–13 (cf. Rashi).

16. The reading שכרו in MS Vat. Ebr. 111 is clearly an error.

17. Presumably he indicates his acceptance in a formal declaration.

18. B. Yevamot 47b indicates that the Palestinian amora Rabbi Yoḥanan required three and even directed the tanna (memorizer) in his academy to emend the text of the *baraita'* to say three. Cf. also B. Yevamot 46b. It is most likely that the tannaitic *halakhah* required only two while the amoraim required three. The tannaim saw the function of these scholars as witnesses and so required two, while the amoraim saw it as that of a court, the minimum size of which was three. It is only with such witnesses or in the presence of a court that conversion is valid, specifically

because the convert is joining the Jewish people, not simply expressing his willingness to believe in the Torah of God. He makes a covenant with both God *and* the nation of Israel. The scholars serve as the representatives of the Jewish people in admitting the proselyte.

19. MS Munich: עומדין לו על גבו.

20. Note that the text says כישראל, and not simply ישראל. This is probably because there are certain small differences between the legal status of an Israelite and that of a convert, most important of which is that a convert may marry certain classes prohibited to Israelites.

21. MS Munich omits נשים.

22. For reasons of modesty.

23. A similar phenomenon regarding the instruction of new members of the Qumran sect is observed in my *Sectarian Law in the Dead Sea Scrolls, Courts, Testimony and the Penal Code* (1983), pp. 156–9.

24. As reconstructed by Lieberman: גר שקיבל עליו כל דברי תורה חוץ מדבר אחד אין מקבלין אותו. ר' יוסה בי ר' יהודה או': אפ' דבר קטן מדקדוקי סופרים. This reconstruction is supported by parallels (see Lieberman, *TK,* ad loc.), especially *Sifra',* ed. Weiss, p. 91a.

25. The entire first clause is accidently omitted in MS Vienna (Lieberman).

26. This is the reading of MS Vienna. MS Erfurt: אחד.

27. Rashi (B. Bekhorot 30b) explains *diqduq soferim* as a stringency of the Rabbis.

28. B. Shabbat 31a. Cf. Bamberger, pp. 223–5.

29. While it is difficult to date this narrative, we should note that it indicates that the tannaim dated the dual-Torah concept as far back as the time of Hillel and Shammai.

30. J. Neusner, "Rabbinic Traditions about the Pharisees before A.D. 70: The Problem of Oral Transmission," *JJS* 22 (1971), pp. 1–18, argues for a Yavnean date. He is certainly correct that the dual-Torah concept is unattested before Yavneh, but we would view it as the result of a long and complex prehistory and would see it developing into its present form in the second half of the first century C.E.

31. Cf. Bamberger, pp. 225–8, and my *"Ha-Giyyur,"* pp. 258f., 260.

32. Cf. B. Yevamot 71b–72a and the commentary of David Kimhi to Josh. 5:2.

33. Herodotus, *Historiae* II, 104:1–3. Cf. the comments of M. Stern, *Greek and Latin Authors on Jews and Judaism* I (1976), pp. 2–4.

34. J. Licht, *"Milah,"* *'Enṣiqlopedyah Miqra'it* IV, 896–8. It is uncertain whether circumcision in Egypt was practiced by all classes or only by certain groups.

35. M. Stern, *Greek and Latin Authors* I, 169f., 225, 300, 312, 315 (although the Jews never practiced female circumcision), 325, 356, 415, 436, 442–4, 525f., 528. The second most prominent sign was Sabbath observance. Sabbath observance, moreover, was much more widespread among non-Jews in the Greco-Roman period than was circumcision.

36. E. M. Smallwood, "The Legislation of Hadrian and Antoninus Pius against Circumcision," *Latomus* 18 (1959), pp. 334–47.

37. Lieberman, *TK,* ad loc. and Smallwood, "The Legislation of Hadrian and Antoninus Pius against Circumcision: Addendum," *Latomus* 20 (1961), pp. 93–96.

38. Bamberger, pp. 21f. Cf. Gen. 34:14–24.

39. For full discussion, see Licht, 898–900.

40. E.g. K. Kohler, "Circumcision," *JE* IV, p. 94.

41. See above, n. 35 and Belkin, *Philo and the Oral Law,* p. 47.

42. See my *"Ha-Giyyur,"* pp. 259, 260f.

43. H. H. Rowley, "Jewish Proselyte Baptism and the Baptism of John," *From Moses to Qumran* (1963), pp. 225f. The article originally appeared in *HUCA* 15 (1940), pp. 313–34. Cf. I. Abrahams, *Studies in Pharisaism and the Gospels* (1967), 1st Series, pp. 36–46.

44. See the exhaustive study of A. Büchler, "The Levitical Impurity of the Gentile in Palestine before the year 70," *JQR* n.s. 17 (1926/7), pp. 1–81. He argues that the origin of these laws is in the period immediately preceding the outbreak of the revolt in 66 C.E. (pp. 1–3, 80).

45. Bamberger, pp. 43f.; Rowley, pp. 227–30.

46. Rowley, pp. 211–35. Contrast D. Flusser, *"Tevilat Yoḥanan We-Khat Midbar Yehudah,"* *Yahadut U-Meqorot Ha-Naṣerut* (1979), pp. 81–112.

47. So Bamberger, p. 44.

48. MS Kaufmann: גר שניתגייר ערב פסחים, בית שמי או': טובל ואוכל את פסחו לערב. ובית הלל או': הפורש מן העורלה כפורש מן הקבר. MS Munich preserves only orthographic variants. This mishnah also appears in M. ʿEduyot 5:2. The reading פסח for פסחים seems to have originated in *ed. princ.* It probably is a misinterpretation of an abbreviation. Cf. G. Alon, *"Ṭum'at Nokhrim," Meḥqarim Be-Toledot Yisra'el* (1967) I, pp. 121–47, translated in G. Alon, *Jews, Judaism and the Classical World* (1977), pp. 146–89. Alon argues for an early dating of proselyte immersion, which he understands to be based on the general concept of the impurity of the Gentiles which in his view predates the Herodian period. Alon sees proselyte immersion as predating Christian baptism, although to him the character of each is markedly different.

49. Purification from the impurity of the dead involved sprinkling of the water (in which ashes of the burnt red heifer were mixed) on the third and seventh days.

50. Maimonides, H. Qorban Pesaḥ 6:7, clarifies the view of the Hillelites. He asks how it is possible to stop the new proselyte from eating the paschal sacrifice (a commandment of the Torah punishable by excision) in order to prevent an error in later years (a Rabbinic ordinance). He answers that the Hillelites did not allow one circumcised so close to Passover to immerse for purposes of conversion, so that he would not attain Jewish status until after the paschal sacrifices were eaten. In other words, they made sure that the conflict between the Torah's law and their ordinance would never occur.

51. MS Vienna, ed. Lieberman: אמ' ר' לעזר בי ר' צדוק: מחדין בית שמיי ובית הלל בערל אמ' ר' לעזר בי ר' צדוק: מחדין בית שמיי ובית הלל בערל זכר שמקבל הזאה ואוכל. על מה נחלקו? על ערל גוי. שבית שמיי או': טובל ואוכל את פסחו לערב. ובית הלל או': הפורש מן הערלה כפורש מן הקבר. אחד נכרי שמל ואחת שפחה שטבלה. ר' ליעזר בן יעקב או': אצטדריוטות ושומרי ציירין היו בירושלם שטובלין ואוכלין פסחיהן לערב.

52. MS Erfurt: יוסה בר' יהודה, MS London: יוסי.

53. MS Erfurt: לא נחלקו. D. Halivni, *Meqorot U-Mesorot, Mo'ed* (1974/5), pp. 284, 302 shows that the phrase *lo' neḥelequ* can be taken to mean that according to either the tanna or the redactor of the statement there was another view, to the effect that "they did argue." In our case, this may mean that there was an opposing view which stated that there was a dispute between the Houses of Hillel and Shammai as to whether a Jew circumcised on the day before Passover might eat of the paschal lamb that year.

54. MSS Erfurt and London and *ed. princ.*: זר, but Lieberman, *TK,* ad loc., shows conclusively that the reading of MS Vienna is to be preferred.

55. *Ed. princ.*: בר' צדוק, clearly an error which simply repeated the name of the last tanna cited.

56. στρατιῶται (Lieberman, *TK,* ad loc.).

57. See Lieberman, *TK,* ad loc.

58. The specific mention of the handmaiden is, according to Lieberman, indication that our tosefta is based on a specific *midrash halakhah*. See *TK,* ad loc.

59. *Tevilah,* from the root *ṭbl.*

60. *Hazzayah* or *hazza'ah* from the root *nzh.*

61. See n. 52 and Lieberman, *TK,* ad loc.

62. S. Zeitlin, "The Halaka in the Gospels and its Relation to the Jewish Law in the Time of Jesus," *HUCA* 1 (1924), pp. 357–63, and "A Note on Baptism for Proselytes," *JBL* 52 (1933), pp. 78f., has dated immersion to a very late date. Cf. the response of L. Finkelstein, "The Institution of Baptism for Proselytes," *JBL* 52 (1933), pp. 203–11. See also my *"Ha-Giyyur,"* p. 282, in which it is suggested that the immersion is not mentioned in the account preserved in Josephus of the conversion of the royal house of Adiabene perhaps because the immersion took place only in connection with the sacrificial offering. Since the description in Josephus' source is written from the point of view of the affairs of Adiabene, immersion would not have been mentioned or, perhaps, even known. If so, we might explain that Helena and the sons of Izates did eventually immerse upon their arrival in Jerusalem as a precondition for the offering of the proselyte's sacrifice.

63. MS Kaufmann: ארבעה מחוסרי כיפורים . . . הזב והזבה והיולדת והמצורע. ר' אליעזר בן יעקב אומ': גר מחוסר כיפורין עד שיזרק עליו הדם, ונזיר . . . . Cf. J. Neusner, *A History of the Mishnaic Law of Holy Things* V (1980), pp. 19f.

64. See J. Preuss, *Biblical and Talmudic Medicine,* trans F. Rosner (1978), pp. 354–7.

65. Preuss, pp. 375f.

66. Because of the difficulties in identifying the disease *ṣara'at,* so often explained as leprosy, we leave this word untranslated. See Y. Tass, "*Ṣara'at*" sec. d, *'Enṣiqlopedyah Miqra'it* VI, 776–8, and Preuss, pp. 323–39. Preuss's discussion of this disease is outdated, and the view of Tass is to be preferred.

67. So I. Lipschutz, *Tiferet Yisra'el,* ad loc. Cf. Maimonides, H. Meḥussere Kapparah 1:1.

68. Cf. B. Levine, "Kippurim," *Eretz Israel* 9 (1969), pp. 88–95.

69. A. Hyman, *Toledot Tanna'im We-'Amora'im* (1963/4), pp. 181–4.

70. So Lieberman, *TK,* to T. Pesaḥim 7:14.

71. Cf. my "*Ha-Giyyur,*" pp. 259, 262.

72. MS Munich: כבר נמנה עליה תנו רבנן: גר בזמן הזה צריך שיפריש רובע לקינו. א״ר שמעון: רבן יוחנן בן זכאי ובטל׳ מפני התקלה. The *baraita'* is also found in B. Rosh Ha-Shanah 31b. This *baraita'* is in agreement with the anonymous first clause of M. Keritot 2:1, for it is precisely because the proselyte is not in the category of one lacking in atonement that the tannaim strove at first to preserve some means of making the offering. After all, the offering was essential to the conversion process. In the view of Rabbi Eliezer ben Jacob, that the convert is simply "lacking in atonement," the offering would have no purpose after the destruction of the Temple. Gerim 2:4 seems to have misunderstood this. It construes Rabbi Eliezer ben Jacob as stating that the convert must still set aside the money for the offering. But to Rabbi Eliezer there is absolutely no reason to do so since the purpose of the offering no longer existed after the destruction. On the contrary, Rabbi Eliezer ben Jacob in M. Keritot is in accord with the view which Gerim 2:4 ascribes to Rabbi Simeon, that one simply need not bring the offering.

73. *Ba-zeman ha-zeh* is a technical term for the period after the destruction of the Temple. It is almost always used in reference to problems of adapting *halakhah* to fit the new circumstances in which there were no Temple and sacrifices. The impact of the destruction on numerous areas of ritual cannot be overstated.

74. So Rashi to B. Keritot 9a in accordance with B. Keritot 10b. But Rashi to B. Rosh Ha-Shanah 31b, basing himself on B. Yoma' 55b, says it is a quarter sheqel, which would be twice as much. Tosafot to B. Rosh Ha-Shanah 31b suggests that the value rose as a result of inflation.

75. B. Rosh Ha-Shanah 31b: שמעון בן אלעז׳ (ed. Venice). Cf. *Diqduqe Soferim,* ad loc.

76. See also MS Vat. Ebr. 110 and B. Rosh Ha-Shanah 31b, although ed. Vilna reads עליו. If the pronoun refers to the *baraita'* or *halakhah* as understood object, a feminine form would be more correct.

77. See above, n. 75.

78. Such *baraitot* were often formulated or taught by the amoraim in whose names they are handed down. The amoraim viewed such *baraitot* as having less authority than those transmitted in the name of tannaim but as being more

authoritative than amoraic material. See Ch. Albeck, *Meḥqarim Bi-Baraita' We-Tosefta' We-Yaḥasan La-Talmud* (1969), pp. 15–43. In the case of Bar Kappara, we should also remember that he was one of those transitional individuals who bridged the period of the tannaim and the amoraim and can be regarded simultaneously as both a tanna and an amora. See Y. D. Gilat, "Bar Kappara'," *EJ* IV, 227f.

79. Ed. Venice: ת״ר: גר שמל ולא טבל, ר׳ אליעזר אומר הרי זה גר, שכן מצינו באבותינו שמלו ולא טבלו. טבל ולא מל, רבי יהושע אומר הרי זה גר, שכן מצינו באימהות שטבלו ולא מלו. וחכמים אומ׳: טבל ולא מל, מל ולא טבל, אין גר עד שימל ויטבול. No significant variants were found in MS Munich or MS Vat. Ebr. 111. Cf. Neusner, *Eliezer ben Hyrcanus* (1973) I, p. 180; II, p. 409, and Y. D. Gilat, *Mishnato shel R. 'Eli'ezer ben Hyrcanus* (1968), p. 163.

80. Regarding the "fathers" and "mothers" who left Egypt, see above, p. 19.

81. Ed. Venice: ...תני: גר שמל ולא טבל, טבל ולא מל, הכל הולך אחר המילה, דברי רבי אליעזר. רבי יהושע אומר: אף הטבילה מעכבת.

82. Gerim 1:2 (*Sheva' Massekhtot Qeṭanot*, ed. M. Higger [1970/1]) reads עקיבא.

83. Ed. Venice: ...תני בר קפרא: גר שמל ולא טבל הרי זה כשר, שאין גר שלא טבל לקירויו.

84. MS. Leiden adds: טבל ולא מל, which has been erased by another hand (J. N. Epstein, *Mevo'ot Le-Sifrut Ha-'Amora'im* [1962], p. 589.) Indeed, the deletion of these words is necessary according to the context.

85. A *genizah* fragment in L. Ginzberg, *Seride Ha-Yerushalmi* (1909) reads: שאינו טובל.

86. This translation is to be preferred to "nocturnal emission" or "nocturnal pollution," as it is more in keeping with the halakhic definition. See *"Ba'al Qeri," 'Enṣiqlopedyah Talmudit* IV, pp. 130–48.

87. See the survey of views in Bamberger, pp. 48f. Cf. my *"Ha-Giyyur,"* p. 261.

88. The gemara (B. Yevamot 46b) interprets the controversy differently in order to explain the reasons given by the *baraita'* for the views of Rabbi Eliezer and Rabbi Joshua. The gemara claims that both of them agreed (*Kuleh 'alma'* here includes both of them but cannot include the view of the sages) that one who immersed but was not circumcised was a valid proselyte. The disagreement was only regarding one who was circumcised but did not immerse. Rabbi Eliezer considers him a valid proselyte while Rabbi Joshua does not. *Tosefot Yeshanim*, ad loc. (cf. *Tosafot* as well) perceived that this interpretation does not fit the language of the *baraita'* at all. *Tosefot Yeshanim* explains away this problem by saying that the view of Rabbi Joshua was formulated as it is only because of the need to accommodate the phraseology of the entire *baraita'* to the view of the sages that both circumcision and immersion are required. Since we see the reasons as a secondary addition to the *baraita',* we cannot accept the gemara's casuistic reinterpretation of the *baraita'* to suit the reasons. As to the explanation of the Tosafists, the view of the sages was probably also a later addition, since it is not given a reason. It would have followed the addition of the

reasons to the views of Rabbi Eliezer and Rabbi Joshua in the Babylonian recension. If so, it is impossible to believe that the entire *baraita'* was phrased to accord with the view of the sages. For all these reasons, the amoraic explanation of this *baraita'* in the Babylonian gemara cannot be accepted. We should note that this explanation is absent from the Palestinian gemara, where the reasons and the view of the sages are also absent.

89. The Babylonian gemara quotes a second *baraita'* (B. Yevamot 46b), according to which the view of the sages is accepted by Rabbi Yose and that of Rabbi Eliezer by Rabbi Judah. (Cf. D. Halivni, *Meqorot U-Mesorot, Nashim* [1974/5], ad loc.) Rabbi Judah is Judah bar Ilai and Rabbi Yose is Yose bar Halafta. Both of these were third-generation tannaim. It is, therefore, easy to understand why they would echo the views of their second-generation predecessors.

90. *Meqorot U-Mesorot, Nashim*, p. 55 n. 6. Halivni prefaces the explanation with "perhaps."

91. הטבילה מעכבת.

92. אף. Cf. Halivni, *Meqorot U-Mesorot, Mo'ed*, p. 263, and J. N. Epstein, *Mavo' Le-Nusaḥ Ha-Mishnah* (1963/4) II, pp. 1007–32.

93. For similar amoraic statements regarding both men and women, see B. Yevamot 45b and Bamberger, pp. 47f.

94. B. Yevamot 46a–b.

95. Cf. Halivni, *Nashim*, p. 55 n. 6; Bamberger, p. 52.

96. See above, n. 88.

97. *Proselytism*, pp. 51f.

98. On slavery in Second Temple and Rabbinic times, see E. E. Urbach, "*Hilekhot 'Avadim Ke-Maqor Le-Historiyah Ha-Ḥevratit Bi-Yeme Ha-Bayit Ha-Sheni U-Vi-Tequfat Ha-Mishnah We-Ha-Talmud,*" *Zion* 25 (1960), pp. 141–89.

99. For a detailed account, see Bamberger, pp. 124–31. Cf. also Gilat, pp. 162f. Note that this procedure for conversion is mentioned in *Damascus Document* (CDC) 12:10f., which prohibits the selling of male or female slaves who had entered the covenant of Abraham (*'asher ba'u 'immo bi-verit 'avraham*).

100. See, e.g., Maimonides, H. 'Issure Bi'ah 13:12.

101. John Hyrcanus forcibly converted the Edomites to Judaism (Ant. XIII, ix, 1 [257–8]). There is an account which relates that his son Aristobulus I forcibly converted the Itureans (Ant. XIII, xi, 3 [318], although A. Schalit sees this as referring to his father's conquest of the upper Galilee ("Aristobulus I [Judah]," *EJ* III, p. 440).

102. E. Schürer, *A History of the Jewish People in the Time of Jesus Christ* (1891) II, ii, pp. 291–327; Bamberger, pp. 133–8; S. Lieberman, *Greek in Jewish Palestine* (1965), pp. 68–90. I was especially helped by an unpublished seminar paper by Prof. Stuart Miller, now of the University of Connecticut at Storrs, entitled "Proselytes and

God-fearers in Non-Rabbinic Sources of the First Century C.E." (January 1975). Cf. also the material cited in my *"Ha-Giyyur,"* n. 39. The entire issue is in need of reevaluation, as shown by A. T. Kraabel, "The Disappearance of the 'God-Fearers,'" *Numen* 28 (1981), pp. 113–26.

103. By using the term "community" I intend to indicate that the tannaim had a large group of followers among the population of post-70 C.E. Palestine, perhaps including much of the Jewish community. The work of the Rabbis was not limited to the four cubits of the schoolhouse but extended to areas of daily life in which the tannaim functioned as judges, teachers, and religious leaders.

IV.　Heretics and Apostates

1. MS Kaufmann: ואילו שאין להם חלק לעולם הבא: האומר אין תחיית המתים ואין תורה מן השמים, ואפיקורס. While some Mishnah texts begin with the clause stating that all Israel have a share in the world to come, it is clear from the omission of this clause in most manuscripts that it is secondary. We have therefore omitted it from discussion. See Urbach, *Ḥazal,* p. 588 n. 11. L. Finkelstein, *Mavo' Le-Massekhtot 'Avot We-'Avot De-Rabbi Natan* (1950), pp. 104–7, takes the view that the original place of this clause and the entire Sanhedrin 10:1 was the introduction to M. 'Avot in its early form as a Pharisaic document. There is, however, simply no way of proving this ingenious theory.

2. Other texts read אלו. It might be objected that the *waw* of ואלו might indicate that it was preceded by the clause concerning the portion of all Israel (above, n. 1), the *waw* serving as the *waw* of contrast meaning "but." On the other hand, all the previous chapters begin with *we-'elu.* Rather, we should see the *waw* here as functioning much like Arabic *fa.* Cf. Halivni, *Meqorot U-Mesorot, Mo'ed,* p. 526 n. 2**.

3. On חלק, see Finkelstein, p. 221, who sees the usage here in a temporal rather than a spatial sense. He understands the word to mean "future," or "lot."

4. On the world to come and its various definitions in Rabbinic and medieval Judaism, see Finkelstein, pp. 213–21.

5. The words מן התורה are added in many texts. Nonetheless, they must be seen as a late addition (Finkelstein, p. 229). The addition was probably made under the influence of the many *midrashim* attempting to establish the basis of this concept in the Bible. The quotation of this mishnah in P. Pe'ah 1:1 (16b) shows that מן התורה was not part of the original text.

6. Transliterated in accord with the vocalization of MS Kaufmann. Cf. E. Ben-Yehudah, *Millon Ha-Lashon Ha-'Ivrit* (1959) I, p. 349 n. 1.

7. See A. Hyman, "Maimonides' 'Thirteen Principles,'" *Jewish Medieval and Renaissance Studies,* ed. A. Altmann (1967), pp. 119–44. For a general bibliography on dogma and creed in Judaism, see Hyman, p. 120 n. 7.

8. The view expressed here is effectively a compromise between the two possibilities discussed in Hyman, pp. 122f. On the one hand, it is difficult to accept the view of Maimonides and Joseph Albo that one must affirm these beliefs to have a share in the world to come. On the other hand, Hyman's assumption that on the surface there is no relation between this mishnah and required belief is overstated, especially when one takes into consideration the tenuous relationship of the statement "All Israel has a share in the world to come" to the rest of the mishnah. See above, n. 1.

9. Ed. Venice: שכל תנא: הוא כפר בתחיית המתים. לפיכך, לא יהיה לו חלק בתחיית המתים.
... מידותיו של הקב"ה מידה כנגד מידה.

10. MS Munich here reads לעול' הבא, but MS Florence accords with Ed. Venice. R. N. Rabbinovicz, *Diqduqe Soferim*, ad loc., prefers the reading of the printed editions. Indeed, it seems that the version of MS Munich has substituted the interpretation for the text itself. Cf. *Ḥiddushe Rabbenu David Bonfil*, ed. Y. Lipshitz (1966/7), p. 79, and (pseudo-) Ran (Nissim ben Reuven Gerondi), ad loc.

11. On the principle of מידה כנגד מידה, see E. Urbach, *Ḥazal*, pp. 325f., 386f.

12. War II, viii, 14 (164–5). Cf. Ant. XVIII, i, 4 (16), and Schürer (1891) II, ii, pp. 13f.

13. Finkelstein, p. 228.

14. See J. Neusner, "Rabbinic Traditions about the Pharisees before A.D. 70: The Problem of Oral Transmission," *JJS* 22 (1971), pp. 1–18.

15. But cf. Urbach, *Ḥazal*, pp. 254–8. If the wider use of Torah could be proven for pre-70 C.E. Palestine, we would say that the "Torah" in our mishnah and M. 'Avot 1:1 is meant to include the "traditions of the elders" ascribed by Josephus to the Pharisees. These traditions were a forerunner of the tannaitic oral Law.

16. A. J. Heschel, *Torah min Ha-Shamayim Ba-'Aspaqlaryah shel Ha-Dorot* (1965) II, pp. 100–45.

17. Cf. V. Tcherikover, *Hellenistic Civilization and the Jews* (1966), pp. 152–74.

18. S. Krauss, *Griechische und Lateinische Lehnwörter im Talmud, Midrasch und Targum* (1964), II, p. 107.

19. B. Sanhedrin 99b–100a, P. Sanhedrin 10:1 (27d). Cf. "'Apiqoros," 'Enṣiqlopedyah Talmudit II, pp. 136f., which also contains an excellent survey of the medieval halakhic discussion.

20. Cf. Maimonides, *Perush Ha-Mishnayot*, ad loc. (ed. Vilna, p. 124), who derives the word from Aramaic פקר.

21. Ant. X, xi, 7 (277–8). Cf. G. Deutsch, "Apiḳoros," *JE* 1, pp. 665f., and S. Lieberman, "How Much Greek in Jewish Palestine?" *Biblical and Other Studies*, ed. A. Altmann (1963), p. 130.

22. On these beliefs of Epicurus, see J. M. Rist, *Epicurus* (1972), pp. 146–8, and G. Strodach, *The Philosophy of Epicurus* (1963), pp. 52–55.

23. War II, viii, 14 (164–5); Ant. XIII, v, 9 (173).

24. Schürer (1891) II, ii, p. 15.

25. L. Finkelstein sees our mishnah as part of an ancient Pharisaic document going back as far as the "Men of the Great Assembly," a view which we find difficult to accept. He sees the specific passage under discussion here, however, as being a later addition. At the same time, he suggests that it must have been added at a time when Epicureanism was making inroads into the Jewish people. Unfortunately, however, it is not possible to determine precisely the status of Epicurean beliefs among Jews at this time so as to date more exactly the formulation of our mishnah.

26. Accordingly, the word "even" (Hebrew *'af*) in our passage should be understood as part of the words of the tannaim Rabbi Akiva and Abba Saul rather than as an addition of some redactor, as was the case in the passage discussed above. Cf. p. 34.

27. MS. Vienna: אבל המינין והמשומדין והמסורות ואפיקורוסיים והכופרין בתורה ופורשי מדרכי צבור ושאין מודין בתחיית המתים, וכל מי שחטא והחטיא את הרבים ,,. . . גיהנם נתנעלת בפניהם ודונין בה לדורי דורות . . . . Cf. B. Rosh Ha-Shanah 17a, ed. Venice, and *Diqduqe Soferim,* ad loc., as well as the discussion in R. T. Herford, *Christianity in the Talmud and Midrash* (1975), pp. 118–25.

28. According to Rashi to B. Rosh Ha-Shanah 17a, in the version of *Diqduqe Soferim,* the *minim* here are the *talmide yeshu,* the disciples of Jesus, in other words, the early Jewish Christians.

29. ופורשי מדרכי צבור is too general a classification to belong to this list. Delete it with Rashi and *Diqduqe Soferim* to B. Rosh Ha-Shanah 17a.

30. MS Erfurt (ed. Zuckermandel): ושכפרו בתחיית המתים.

31. The text here mentions Jeroboam and Ahab and then adds two classes of transgressors extremely difficult to explain precisely and not relevant to our study.

32. See B. Kedar, "Netherworld, In the Aggadah," *EJ* XII, 997f. for a treatment of Gehenna in Rabbinic texts.

33. Contrast, however, the view of Rashi to B. Rosh Ha-Shanah 17a who sees the offense of the informer as causing financial loss to fellow Jews.

34. The printed editions of Rabbinic texts usually read *mumar,* lit. "one who was changed" or converted, for the Hebrew *meshummad,* lit. "one who was destroyed." Christian censors replaced *meshummad* with *mumar,* which they deemed less offensive. Indeed, the word *mumar* itself is most probably an invention of the Christian censors. Cf. [N.] Porges, *"Der Talmud Jeruschalmi zu Chullin und Bechoroth,"* *ZHB* 11 (1907), p. 158; the response of W. Bacher, *"Der Ausdruck* מומָר *in den Handschriften des Talmuds,"* *ZHB* 12 (1908), pp. 39f.; and the reply of [N.] Porges, *Zum Ausdruck* מומָר *in den Handschriften des Talmuds,"* *ZHB* 12 (1908), pp. 108–110. See also S. Lieberman, "Some Aspects of After Life in Early Rabbinic Literature," *Texts and Studies* (1974), pp. 531f.

35. TK III, p. 402 n. 45.

36. Ed. Venice: תנו רבנן: אכל חלב, זהו משומד. ואיזהו משומד? אכל נבילות וטריפות, שקצים

The version in T. Horayot ורמשים ושתה יין נסך. רבי יוסי ברבי יהודה אומר: אף הלובש כלאים.
1:5, MS Vienna reads: האוכל שקצין, הרי זה משומד. כיצד משומד? אכל נבלות וטרפות, שקצים
ורמשים, האוכל בשר חזיר והשותה יין נסך, והמחלל את השבת והמשוך. ר' יוסי בר' יהודה אר': אף
הלובש כלאים. ר' שמעון בן לעזר אום': אף העושה דבר שאין היצר תאב לו.

37. MS Munich reads: אוכל ... והשותה (*Diqduqe Soferim,* ad loc.).

38. I.e. an animal that would have died of itself if not slaughtered ritually. Such animals are termed *ṭerefot,* literally "torn animals," and are forbidden according to *halakhah.*

39. Translating with Jastrow s.v.

40. The reading ר' יהודה found in some late printed texts is clearly an error. See *Diqduqe Soferim,* ad loc.

41. Generally termed *sha'aṭnez* and prohibited according to Lev. 19:19 and Deut. 22:11.

42. The redactor of the *baraita'* in its present form added the *waw* before *'ezehu* which stood in the material before him in order to ease the transition. Nevertheless, the awkwardness as well as the apparent redundancy of the formulation give evidence of its building blocks. Indeed, this redundancy was felt by the amoraim who interpreted the first clause to refer to the *meshummad* and the second to the *min.*

43. *Sifra'* Wa-Yiqra', Parashah 2:3 (ed. Weiss, p. 4b): אדם: לרבות את הגרים. מכם:
להוציא את המשומדים. ... ת"ל בני ישראל. ... מה ישראל מקבלי ברית, אף הגרים מקבלי ברית. יצאו
המשומדים שאינן מקבלי ברית שהרי הפרו ברית.... On this passage see E. P. Sanders, *Paul and Palestinian Judaism* (1977), pp. 83f. Cf. P. Sheqalim 1:4 (ed. Krot. 1:5, 46b).

44. Reading מקבלי ברית with Weiss and MS Rome, Assemani 66 (ed. Finkelstein, 1956).

45. Ed. Venice: מכם: לא כולכם, להוציא את המשומד. מכם: בכם חלקתי ולא באומר. מן
הבהמה: להביא בני אדם שדומים לבהמה. מכאן אמרו: מקבלין קרבנות מפושעי ישראל כדי שיחזרו בהן
בתשובה, חוץ מן המשומד ומנסך את היין ומחלל שבתו בפרהסיא.

46. MSS Hamburg and Rome (a) add מכם a second time (*Diqduqe Soferim,* ad loc.).

47. All MSS read הדומין (*Diqduqe Soferim,* ad loc.).

48. Cf. עם הדומה לחמור in B. Yevamot 62a, *Midrash Tanḥuma'* Wa-Yera' 46 (ed. Buber, p. 57a), and the note of Buber, ad loc.; and *Bereshit Rabbah* 56:2 (ed. Theodor-Albeck II, p. 596), and the parallels cited by Theodor, ad loc.

49. See D. Halivni, "Yesh Mevi'im Bikkurim," *Bar-'Ilan* 7–8 (1969/70), p. 79.

50. On *poshe'e yisra'el* in later texts, cf. A. Marmorstein, "Judaism and Christianity in the Middle of the Third Century," *HUCA* 10 (1935), pp. 223–63.

51. Two more passages show that the tannaim did not consider the *meshummadim,* or for that matter any other transgressors, as non-Jews. Instead they are listed separately from the *goyim,* the non-Jews. See B. Avodah Zarah 26a–b and B. Giṭṭin 45b. On apostates in the writings of Philo, see H. Wolfson, *Philo I* (1968), pp. 73–85.

V. *Tannaitic Judaism and the Early Christians*

1. See M. Smith, *Jesus the Magician* (1978), pp. 1–67 for a thorough study of the early anti-Christian polemic.

2. Maimonides, H. Melakhim 11:3, states that Rabbi Akiva and his contemporaries erred in thinking Bar Kokhba (Bar Kosiba) to be the Messiah. Needless to say, no accusation of heresy was lodged against these scholars.

3. S. W. Baron, *A Social and Religious History of the Jews* II (1952), p. 129. The divisions during the revolt are well documented in D. Rhoads, *Israel in Revolution, 6–74 C.E.* (1976), pp. 94–149.

4. It is usually maintained that the early Christian community of Jerusalem escaped the destruction by fleeing Jerusalem to Pella in Trans-Jordan. If so, this would be evidence that already by this time the Jewish Christians saw themselves as separate at least from the revolutionary faction of the Jewish people. However, recent scholarship has called into question the historicity of this tradition, seeing it instead as an attempt by what are usually called Jewish Christians (which we prefer to term Judaizing Christians) in the region of Pella to trace their ancestry and hence authority to the early Jerusalem Jewish Christian church. See G. Lüdemann, "The Successors of Pre-70 Jerusalem Christianity: A Critical Evaluation of the Pella-Tradition," *Self-Definition* I, pp. 161–173, 245–54.

5. According to Acts 6:7, the "number of disciples multiplied greatly in Jerusalem" (RSV). Nevertheless, the picture one gets from Acts is of a small, close-knit group.

6. See F. F. Bruce, *New Testament History* (1972), pp. 279–90; J. Weiss, *Earliest Christianity* (1959) I, pp. 258–76.

7. Cf. Bruce, pp. 265–78; Weiss I, p. 265.

8. D. Sperber, "Min," *EJ* XII, 1–3.

9. Herford, pp. 361–97, G. Alon, *Toledot Ha-Yehudim Be-'Ereṣ Yisra'el Bi-Tequfat Ha-Mishnah We-Ha-Talmud* (1967) I, pp. 179–92.

10. Cf. I. Elbogen, *Ha-Tefillah Be-Yisra'el* (1972), pp. 27–9, 31, 40; G. Forkman, *The Limits of the Religious Community* (1972), pp. 90–92; P. Schäfer, *Studien zur Geschichte und Theologie des Rabbinischen Judentums* (1978), pp. 45–55 (especially the bibliography in note 3); R. Kimelman, "*Birkat Ha-Minim* and the Lack of Evidence for an Anti-Christian Jewish Prayer in Late Antiquity," *Self-Definition* II, pp. 226–44, 391–403 (which was contributed to the McMaster volume but was not read at the symposium); E. E. Urbach, "Self Isolation or Self Affirmation in Judaism in the First Three Centuries: Theory and Practice," *Self Definition* II, 288–93 and 415f.; and the somewhat tendentious treatment of A. Finkel, "Yavneh's Liturgy and Early Christianity," *Journal of Ecumenical Studies* 18 (1981), pp. 231–46.

11. Cited here from ed. Venice 30a: תנו רבנן: שמעון הפקולי הסדיר שמנה עשרה ברכות

לפני ר"ג על הסדר ביבנה. אמר להם ר"ג לחכמים: כלום יש אדם שיודע לתקן ברכת המינין? עמד שמואל הקטן ותקנה. לשנה אחרת שכחה והשקיף בה שתים ושלש שעות ולא העלוהו. Cf. B. Megillah 17b and Herford, pp. 125–35.

12. MS Munich: סדר.

13. ברכות is omitted in MS Munich.

14. This is in accord with the view that the Men of the Great Assembly composed, but did not place in order, the Eighteen Benedictions (L. Ginzberg, *Perushim We-Ḥiddushim Bi-Yerushalmi* I (1941), p. 332; D. Halivni, *Meqorot U-Mesorot, Mo'ed*, p. 489.

15. Contrast M. Ydit, "Birkat Ha-Minim," *EJ* IV, 1035, who says that Samuel Ha-Qaṭan "revised its text after it had fallen into oblivion." This is impossible in light of the use of the verb *tqn*, which refers to composition or formulation of a text.

16. MS Florence and some *rishonim* read ירד (*Diqduqe Soferim*, ad loc.). This reading seems to be influenced by the continuation of the *baraita'*, which is set in a liturgical context, for *yrd* is a technical term for serving as precentor (*yrd* followed by *lifne ha-tevah*, "to go down before the ark"). Indeed, the precentors in early synagogues stood at a level below that of the worshippers. We, however, prefer the reading *'md*. The first part of the *baraita'* takes place in the setting of the academy at Yavneh where Rabban Gamliel sought a tanna to compose a benediction against *minim*. The following year, Samuel Ha-Qaṭan's "amnesia" occurred in liturgical context as he was serving as precentor. This view is supported by P. Berakhot 5:3 (ed. Krot. 5:4, 9c).

17. While it seems from context that he forgot the text of this blessing, an amoraic passage in P. Berakhot 5:3 (ed. Krot. 5:4, 9c) suggests that he skipped the entire blessing.

18. P. Berakhot 5:3 (ed. Krot. 5:4, 9c) in its Aramaic version of our *baraita'* reads משקיף עליהן, "he looked at them." Ginzberg IV (1961), p. 276, takes this as indicating that the correct reading is the Hebrew עליהם. More probably, the amoraim were confused by this strange use of the *hif'il* of *šqf* and so modified the object pronoun. The word *bah* clearly refers to the benediction.

19. MS Munich: יותר משתים.

20. Literally, "bring him up." Cf. n. 16.

21. Hyman III, p. 1148. Hyman failed to realize that the stories about Samuel Ha-Qaṭan and Hillel are apocryphal.

22. S. Kanter, *Rabban Gamaliel II: The Legal Traditions* (1980), pp. 9f.

23. I. Heinemann, *Ha-Tefillah Bi-Tequfat Ha-Tanna'im We-Ha-'Amora'im* (1966), p. 142, and Lieberman, *TK* I, 53f.

24. Cf. *Midrash Tanḥuma'*, ed. Buber, Lev., p. 2a.

25. למשומדים אל תהי תקוה אם לא ישובו לתורתיך. הנוצרים והמינים כרגע יאבדו. מהרה ימחו מסיפר החיים ועם צדיקים אל יכתיבו. בא"י מכניע זידים (J. Mann, "Genizah Fragments of the

Palestinian Order of Service," *HUCA* 2 [1925], p. 306, restored in accord with S. Schechter, "Genizah Specimens," *JQR* o.s. 10 [1898], pp. 657, 659.)

26. Cf. A. Marmorstein, "The Amidah of the Public Fast Days," *JQR* n.s. 15 (1924), pp. 415–7.

27. See D. M. Smith, "John, Gospel of," *IDB* Supplementary Volume, pp. 482–6, and W. A. Meeks, "Am I a Jew? Johanine Christianity and Judaism," *Christianity, Judaism and other Greco-Roman Cults, Studies for Morton Smith at Sixty,* Part I (1975), pp. 163–86.

28. Cf. the more skeptical approach of Kimelman, pp. 234f.

29. See also Luke 6:22, Forkman 105f., and S. Krauss, "The Jews in the Works of the Church Fathers," *JQR* o.s. 5 (1893), pp. 130–4.

30. Ἀπεκτείνατε γὰρ τὸν δίκαιον, καὶ πρὸ αὐτοῦ τοὺς προφήτας αὐτοῦ καὶ νῦν τοὺς ἐλπίζοντας ἐπ' αὐτόν, καὶ τὸν πέμψαντα αὐτὸν παντοκράτορα καὶ ποιητὴν τῶν ὅλων Θεὸν ἀθετεῖτε, καὶ, ὅσον ἐφ' ὑμῖν, ἀτιμάζετε, καταρώμενοι ἐν ταῖς συναγωγαῖς ὑμῶν τοὺς πιστεύοντας ἐπὶ τὸν Χριστόν.

31. Καὶ τοὺς ἀπὸ τοῦ σπέρματος τοῦ Ἀβραὰμ ζῶντας κατὰ τὸν νόμον, καὶ ἐπὶ τοῦτον τὸν Χριστὸν μὴ πιστεύοντας πρὶν τελευτῆς τοῦ βίου, οὐ σωθήσεσθαι ὁμοίως ἀποφαίνομαι, καὶ μάλιστα τοὺς ἐν ταῖς συναγωγαῖς καταναθεματίσαντας καὶ καταναθεματίζοντας ἐπ' αὐτὸν τοῦτον τὸν Χριστόν,....

32. καταρωμένους καὶ τῶν τοῦτον τὸν ἐσταυρωμένον ὑφ' ὑμῶν ἀποδεικνύντων εἶναι τὸν Χριστόν.

33. ἀλλὰ καὶ καταρᾶσθαι αὐτοῦ καὶ τῶν πιστευόντων εἰς αὐτὸν πάντων τολμᾶτε.

34. ὁποῖα διδάσκουσιν οἱ ἀρχισυνάγωγοι ὑμῶν, μετὰ τὴν προσευχήν.

35. *Hom.* II.8 in Ps. 37 (*PG* XII, 1387): *Christus usque in hodiernum diem a Judaeis anathema fiat.* Cf. Kimelman, p. 398 n. 63.

36. Hom. Jer. 18.12: εἰσελθε εἰς τὰς τῶν Ἰουδαίων συναγωγάς, καὶ ἴδε τὸν Ἰησοῦν ὑπ' αὐτῶν τῇ γλώσσῃ τῆς βλασφημίας μαστιγούμενον.

37. Kimelman, p. 236.

38. ἀλλὰ καὶ ἀνιστάμενοι ἔωθεν καὶ μέσης ἡμέρας καὶ περὶ τὴν ἑσπέραν, τρὶς τῆς ἡμέρας ὅτε εὐχὰς ἐπιτελοῦσιν ἑαυτοῖς ἐν ταῖς συναγωγαῖς ἐπαρῶνται αὐτοῖς καὶ ἀναθεματίζουσι, τρὶς τῆς ἡμέρας φάσκοντες ὅτι ,,ἐπικαταράσαι ὁ θεὸς τοὺς Ναζωραίους,,. *Anacephalaiosis* 29.9.1, ed. and trans. in A. F. J. Klijn and G. J. Reinink, *Patristic Evidence for Jewish-Christian Sects* (1973), p. 175.

39. See Klijn and Reinink, pp. 44–52, for a survey of evidence regarding this sect.

40. Klijn and Reinink, p. 219: *... usque hodie in synagogis suis sub nomine Nazarenorum blasphemant populum christianum . . . (in Amos 1, 11–12).* The translation Nazoraeans for Latin *Nazarenorum* in Klijn and Reinink is incorrect as will be noted below.

41. Klijn and Reinink, p. 221: *usque hodie perseuerant in blasphemiis et ter per*

singulos dies in omnibus synagogis sub nomine Nazarenorum anathematizent uocabulum Christianum (in Esaiam 5, 18–19). Cf. n. 40.

42. Klijn and Reinink, pp. 225: *. . . cui ter per singulos dies sub nomine Nazarenorum maledicunt in synagogis suis (in Esaiam 49, 9).* Cf. n. 40.

43. *. . . in synagogis uestris, qui diebus ac noctibus blasphemant Saluatorem, et sub nomine, ut saepe dixi, Nazarenorum, ter in die in Christianos congerunt maledicta (in Esaiam 52, 4–6).*

44. Kimelman, pp. 237–9.

45. Jerome consistently distinguishes between *Nazaraei,* the Jewish Christian sect of the Nazoraeans, and the *Nazareni,* the Nazarenes, a general designation for Christians.

46. *Epistles to Augustine* 112.31: *Usque hodie per totas Orientis synagogas inter Iudaeos haeresis est, quae dicitur Minaeorum, et a Pharisaeis huc usque damnatur: quos uulgo Nazaraeos nuncupant, qui credunt in Christum, Filium Dei, natum de Maria uirgine, et eum dicunt esse, qui sub Pontio Pilato passus est, et resurrexit, in quem et nos credimus: sed dum uolunt et Iudaei esse et Christiani, nec Iudaei sunt, nec Christiani* (Klijn and Reinink, p. 201).

47. Kimelman, pp. 241–4. His philological discussion (pp. 399f. n. 91) is unconvincing.

48. Herford, pp. 344–7.

49. Herford, pp. 171–3.

50. H.-J. Schoeps, *Jewish Christianity* (1969), p. 11, maintains that the Nazoreans were only a branch of the Ebionites, a view with which it is difficult to concur in light of the evidence presented in Klijn and Reinink.

51. Krauss, ibid.

52. The famous statement ישראל אף על פי שחטא ישראל הוא although based on B. Sanhedrin 44a, was not seen as a *halakhah* until much later. See J. Katz, "'Af 'Al Pi She-Ḥaṭa' Yisra'el Hu'," *Tarbiz* 27 (1957/8), pp. 203–17. Katz takes the view that the use of this statement as a halakhic dictum originated with Rashi. On the other hand, halakhic use of the statement appears in *Midrash 'Aggadah,* ed. S. Buber, to Num., p. 162, to indicate that impurity could be contracted by killing a Jewish apostate for he still retained his Jewish identity despite his transgressions. (This reference is noted in D. Halivni, *Meqorot U-Mesorot, Nashim,* p. 67 n. 3.) This tradition is without parallel. Since much of the material in this text comes from the school of Moses Ha-Darshan, it seems that Rashi was only reflecting a usage already prominent in the French exegetical tradition. Rashi did not originate the halakhic use of this sentence. Cf. also J. Katz, *Exclusiveness and Tolerance* (1962), pp. 67–81, and the many medieval responsa he cites; L. Ginzberg, *An Unknown Jewish Sect* (1976), p. 105; and G. Blidstein, "Who is Not a Jew?—The Medieval Discussion," *ILR* 2 (1976), pp. 369–90.

53. The use of bans in Talmudic times was intended as a means of discipline.

Under no circumstances did they imply any effect on the personal status of the person banned, only on the way he and his neighbors related to one another. Cf. Forkman, pp. 92–105.

54. See G. F. Moore, "The Definition of the Jewish Canon and the Repudiation of Christian Scriptures," *The Canon and Masorah of the Hebrew Bible,* ed. S. Leiman (1974), pp. 115–41.

55. MS Vienna, ed. Lieberman: הגליונים וספרי מינין אין מצילין אותן מפני הדליקה אלא
נשרפין במקומן הן והזכרוותיהן. ר׳ יוסי הגלילי אום׳: בחול קודר את הזכרוותיהן וגונזן, ושורף את השאר.
אמ׳ ר׳ טרפון: אקפח את בני שאם יבאו לידי שאשרפם ואת ההזכרות שבהן. שאפי׳ הרודף רודף אחרי
נכנסתי לבית ע״ז ולא נכנסתי לבתיהן. שעובדי ע״ז אין מכירין אותו וכופרין אותו, והללו מכירין אותו
וכופרין בו.... אמ׳ ר׳ ישמעאל: מה אם להטיל שלום בין איש לאשתו אמ׳ המקום ספר שנכתב בקדושה
ימחה על המים, ספרי מינין שמטילין איבה בין ישראל לאביהם שבשמים על אחת כמה וכמה שימחו הן
והזכרוותיהן.... כשם שאין מצילין אותן מפני הדליקה, כך אין מצילין אותן לא מן המפולת ולא מן המים
ולא מכל דבר המאבד אותן. Cf. J. Lightstone, *Yose the Galilean* I (1979), pp. 21–23.

56. MSS Erfurt and London omit מפני הדליקה.

57. So Lieberman, *TK,* ad loc., and S. Leiman, *The Canonization of Hebrew Scripture* (1976), 190f. n. 511. Contrast Urbach, "Self-Isolation," p. 291.

58. This is an oath formula, MS Erfurt: בני.

59. MSS Erfurt and London: שאני שורפן (London omits the א).

60. This Talmudic *rodef,* "pursuer," is chasing his victim in order to kill him.

61. *Bayit,* "house," is probably used here to refer to a temple or house of worship.

62. *Ed. princ.* and MS Erfurt: בו. London omits.

63. Erfurt and London: לעשות (abbreviated in London).

64. Num. 5:23.

65. MS Erfurt: שמי.

66. MS Erfurt adds: וקנאה ותחרות.

67. MSS Erfurt and London: שישרפו, "that they be burned."

68. MS Erfurt: מפני המפלות.

69. MS Erfurt: מפני.

70. Cf. D. Sperber, "Sifrei Ha-Minim, *EJ* 14, 1521.

71. It should be mentioned in passing that Rabbi Ṭarfon is not to be identified with Tryphon, with whom Justin Martyr conducted his dialogue.

72. MS Vienna: הגליונין וספרי המינין אין מטמאין את הידים.... Cf. Herford, pp. 160f.; Leiman, *Canonization,* p. 109 and notes, pp. 160f.; and J. Neusner, *A History of the Mishnaic Law of Purities,* Part 19 (1977), p. 144.

73. Leiman, *Canonization,* pp. 102–20.

74. MS Vienna: בשר שנמצא ביד גוי מותר בהנאה. ביד מין אסור בהנאה. היוצא מבית ע״ז הרי
זה בשר זבחי מתים, מפני שאמרו: שחיטת המין ע״ז ופיתם פת כותי וויינם יין נסך ופירותיהם טבלים
וספריהם ספרי קוסמין ובניהם ממזרין. אין מוכרין להם ואין לוקחין מהן. אין נושאין מהן ואין נותנין להן,

ואין מלמדין את בניהן אומנות. ואין מתרפאין מהן לא רפוי ממן ולא רפוי נפשות. Cf. Herford, p. 177f., and J. Neusner, *A History of the Mishnaic Law of Holy Things,* Part III (1979), pp. 40f.

75. With ed. Vilna מבית המין. If the reading of MS Vienna is accepted, the text would mean that the meat of the *min* is forbidden just as meat from the house of idolatry is forbidden.

76. An expression derived from Ps. 106:28. Cf. M. 'Avodah Zarah 2:3.

77. *Sefer Ha-Razim,* ed. M. Margaliot (1966), is certainly an example of such a *sefer qosemin.* Cf. Margaliot, pp. XV, 14, 20.

78. Perhaps translate, "We do not hold discussions with them." Indeed, S. Lieberman, *Tosefet Rishonim* II (1938), p. 227 quotes such an interpretation, in the name of Rabbi Isaac (ben Moses of Vienna) Or Zarua (c. 1180–c. 1250), from the *Shilte Ha-Gibborim* of Rabbi Joshua Boaz ben Simon Baruch (16th century). (It is not a direct quotation but a summary of the Tosefta.) Cf. B. 'Avodah Zarah 27b. Lieberman notes that the entire clause is omitted from the London MS.

79. For these expressions, see M. 'Avodah Zarah 2:2, M. Nedarim 4:4 (and the sources cited in Albeck's *"Hashlamot We-Tosafot,"* in *Shishah Sidre Mishnah* [1957–59], ad loc.). B. Avodah Zarah 27a–b discusses these terms. Although the gemara eventually concludes that *rippui mamon* refers to healing of animals, whereas *rippui nefashot* refers to the healing of human beings, it seems that the simple meaning is that proposed earlier, to the effect that *rippui mamon* is healing in cases where there is no mortal danger, and *rippui nefashot* involves mortal danger. This view is supported by the version of our *baraita'* found in B. 'Avodah Zarah 27b, *'afillu le-hayye sha'ah.* Cf. Maimonides, H. Roseah U-Shemirat Nefesh 12:9 (*min* appears in uncensored texts), who synthesizes the various views in the gemara.

80. E.g. *Qohelet Rabbah* to Eccl. 1:18.

81. Cf. M. Yevamot 4:13; Herford, pp. 43–45.

82. See M. Smith, *Jesus the Magician* (1978), pp. 46–50.

83. See above, p. 62f.

84. Note the *baraita'* in B. Ḥullin 13a–b which is parallel to our *mi-pene she-'ameru* clause. This proves that this part of the Tosefta passage preexisted the rest and also continued to circulate independently. Note Rashi to Ḥullin 13a, who comments that the passage must concern a *min* who is Jewish. Indeed, the amora Rabbah bar Avuha states on page 13b that the halakhic category *min* does not apply to non-Jews (so Rashi, ad loc.).

85. See below, p. 70.

86. See M. Shevi'it 8:10 and M. 'Avodah Zarah 2:6.

87. We omit from consideration here another tradition which cannot be said definitely to refer to Jewish Christians. T. Bava' Meṣ'ia' 2:33 (MS Erfurt, ed. Zuckermandel) states: המינין והמשומדים והמסורות מורידין ולא מעלין, "as to heretics, apostates,

and informers, we lower (them into a pit) and we do not lift (them) up." Cf. the parallel in B. 'Avodah Zarah 26b (in uncensored texts) and Herford, pp. 173–7, for the amoraic discussion of this *baraita'*. In any case, this tradition indicates the extremes to which the tannaim were willing to go in dealing with *minim*.

VI. The Jewish Christians in Tannaitic Narrative

1. That the three parts circulated individually can be seen from B. 'Avodah Zarah 16b–17a, in which the Rabbi Eliezer story appears, and B. 'Avodah Zarah 27b, in which the latter part of the second halakhic ruling (MS JTS, ed. Abramson) לא ישא אדם ולא יתן עם המינין ואין מתרפאין מהם אפי׳ לחיי שעה appears followed immediately by the supporting Ben Damah narrative. The Ben Damah narrative appears separately in P. 'Avodah Zarah 2:2 (40d–41a) and P. Shabbat 14:4 (14d–15a), without the preceding halakhic ruling. We have already noted the separate circulation of the *mi-pene she-'ameru* clause (without the second *halakhah*) in B. Ḥullin 13a–b (see above V, n. 84). Both narratives appear in expanded form in *Qohelet Rabbah* to Eccl. 1:8. Note that ed. Vilna (pp. 3b–4a) preserves a censored version.

2. MS Vienna: מעשה בר׳ לעזר בן דמה שנשכו נחש. ובא יעקב איש כפר סמא לרפאתו משום ישוע בן פנטרא ולא הניחו ר׳ ישמעאל. אמרו לו, "אי אתה רשאי בן דמה." אמ׳ לו, "אני אביא לך ראיה שירפאני." ולא הספיק להביא ראיה עד שמת. אמ׳ ר׳ ישמעאל, "אשריך בן דמה שיצאת בשלום ולא פרצת גדירן של חכמים. שכל הפורץ גדירן של חכמים, לסוף פורענות באה עליו, שנ׳: ופורץ גדר ישכנו נחש." Cf. Herford, pp. 103–8; G. Porton, *The Traditions of Rabbi Ishmael* I (1976), pp. 170–2; Neusner, *Holy Things* III, p. 41; Smith, *Jesus, p. 48*.

3. Ed. Vilna adds: בן אחותו של ר׳ ישמעאל, but this addition is not present in *ed. princ.* and is clearly influenced by the version of B. 'Avodah Zarah 27b. Ben Damah was indeed the nephew of Rabbi Ishmael and appears to have been younger. Cf. Hyman I, p. 161. Hyman notes that according to *Hekhalot Rabbati* (ed. A. J. Jellinek, *Bet Ha-Midrash* III [1967], chap. 4, p. 86), Rabbi Eleazar ben Damah was among the ten martyred at the hands of the Romans. He proposes emendation there to Rabbi Judah ben Dama'. Note, however, that the version in S. Wertheimer, *Bate Midrashot* I (1967/8), chap. 5, p. 74, has אלעזר, with בן דמה added by several witnesses in the apparatus.

4. A town in Galilee. The reading Sakhanya in amoraic sources (Lieberman, *TR*, ad loc.) results from confusion with the Jacob of Sikhnin mentioned in the next text we will discuss.

5. Emending to פנטירא. On this designation for Jesus, see J. Z. Lauterbach, *Rabbinic Essays* (1951), pp. 532–9; J. Maier, *Jesus von Nazareth in der talmüdischen Überlieferung* (1978), pp. 260–7; D. Rokeah, "Ben Sṭara' Ben Panṭira Hu'," *Tarbiz* 39 (1969/70), pp. 11–15; and Smith, *Jesus*, pp. 46f. The claim of Porton, *Ishmael* I, p. 172, that this name is actually "a corruption of Joshua b. Peraḥia, a noted magician

in rabbinic texts" is unsubstantiated and, in light of the other occurrences of this name, impossible.

6. Emending to אמר לו (so the translation of Neusner, *Holy Things* III, p. 41). The reading אמרו לו found in MS Vienna and Ms Erfurt (ed. Zuckermandel) is probably the result of a misinterpretation of the abbreviation א״ל. Cf. P. 'Avodah Zarah 2:2 (40d) אמר לו ר' ישמעאל (ed. Venice).

7. For an amoraic suggestion of what proof he might have brought, see P. 'Avodah Zarah 2:2 (40d–41a); P. Shabbat 14:4 (14d–15a).

8. An expression for one who escaped heretical beliefs after a brush with them. Cf. B. Ḥagigah 14b (and G. Scholem, *Jewish Gnosticism, Merkabah Mysticism, and Talmudic Tradition* [1965], pp. 14–19), and *Bereshit Rabbah* 39:3 (ed. Theodor-Albeck, p. 367) which implies not only escape from danger but also escape from doubting God's protection.

9. MS Erfurt (ed. Zuckermandel): גזירן. If indeed this reading is in the MS. (Zuckermandel is full of errors), then it is a scribal error, as the text is clearly based on the image of the fence (*gader*), as can be seen from the scriptural prooftext.

10. MT ופרץ.

11. Herford, p. 105.

12. MS Vienna: מעשה בר' ליעזר שנתפס על דברי מינות והעלו אותו לבמה לדון. אמ' לו אותו הגמון, "זקן כמותך יעסוק בדברים הללו?" אמ' לו, "נאמן דיין עלי." כסבור אותו הגמן שלא אמר ר' ליעזר אלא לו, ור' ליעזר לא נתכוון אלא נגד אביו שבשמים. אמ' לו, "הואיל והאמנתני עליך אף אני כך אמרתי: איפשר שהסבות הללו טועים בדברים. דימוס! הרי אתה פטור." וכשנפטר מן הבמה היה מצטער שנתפס על דברי מינות. נכנסו תלמידיו לנחמו ולא קיבל. נכנס ר' עקיבא ואמ' לו, "ר', אומ' לפניך דבר שמא הרי אין אתה מיצר?" אמ' לו, "אמור!" אמ' לו, "שמא אחד מן המינין אמ' לך דבר של מינות והנאך?" אמ', "השמים! הזכרתני. פעם אחת הייתי מהלך באיסתרטיא של ציפורי. מצאתי יעקב איש כפר סכניא ואמ' דבר של מינות משם ישוע בן פנטירא והנאני ונתפשתי על דברי מינות שעברתי על דברי תורה: הרחק מעליה דרכך ואל תקרב אל פתח ביתה, כי רבים חללים הפילה וגו'." שהיה ר' ליעזר אור': לעולם יהא אדם בורח מן הכיעור ומן הדומה לכיעור. Cf. Herford, pp. 137–45; J. Neusner, *Eliezer ben Hyrcanus, The Tradition and the Man* (1973), pp. 400–3; Neusner, *Holy Things* III, pp. 41f.; Rokeah, pp. 9–11; and Finkel, pp. 247–50. Finkel's assumptions about the primary nature of the Babylonian recension are highly questionable.

13. On *davar* in the sense of charge, see my *Sectarian Law in the Dead Sea Scrolls, Courts, Testimony and the Penal Code* (1983), p. 99 n. 6.

14. Rashi's explanation (Ed. Venice and uncensored early editions) that Roman *minim* (*mine romiyyim*) had arrested him in order to force him to join them does not accord at all with the rest of the story. Rather, the passage refers to Roman persecution of Christians as we shall explain below.

15. Greek βῆμα. Cf. M. 'Avodah Zarah 1:7 which prohibits Jewish builders from building a בימה, among other things, for idolators, apparently because of its use for trials. Cf. S. Lieberman, "Roman Legal Institutions in Early Rabbinics and in the Acta Martyrum," *JQR* n.s. 35 (1944), pp. 13, 15f.

16. Greek ἡγεμών.

17. *Ne'eman* is a technical term for a reliable witness (*Sectarian Law*, p. 82 n. 15, and Lieberman, "Roman Legal Institutions," p. 20 n. 36). The intention of Rabbi Eliezer was to give the impression that the testimony of the governor would be sufficient as his defense. After all, the governor himself had immediately realized that it was impossible that a sage such as Rabbi Eliezer would have been involved in Jewish Christianity.

18. Lieberman, *TR* II, p. 227, explains the *sibbot* as gray hairs. Cf. his review of S. Krauss, *Tosefot He-'Arukh Ha-Shalem*, *KS* 14 (1937), pp. 226.

19. Restoring with *ed. princ.* and MS Erfurt, with Lieberman, "Roman Legal Institutions," p. 20 n. 130. Lieberman takes the preceding as a question, "Is it possible. . .?" and is followed by Neusner, *Eliezer* I, p. 400.

20. A Latin technical term for pronouncing a verdict of acquittal.

21. Neusner translates, "camp."

22. Note the wide use of Torah to include the entire Hebrew Bible. Cf. W. Bacher, *'Erkhe Midrash* (1922/3) I, pp. 133f.

23. Neusner, *Eliezer* I, 401; II, 366.

24. Cf. T. Yevamot 4:7; Lieberman, *TK,* ad loc.; and G. Alon, *Meḥqarim Be-Toldedot Yisra'el* I (1967), pp. 282–4.

25. So Lieberman, "Roman Legal Institutions," p. 21, who suggests that the governor was Q. Pompeius Falco (p. 24 n. 152).

26. Herford, pp. 140–2. Cf. Eusebius, *Ecclesiastical History* III, 32.

27. Lieberman, "Roman Legal Institutions," pp. 20–24.

28. Neusner, *Eliezer* II, 366f.

29. Lieberman (p. 22) assumes that the judge actually believed the accusation at first and that his question was intended to be incriminating. Rabbi Eliezer's response, however, seems to indicate that he himself detected that the governor did not believe the charges.

30. A. Büchler, "The Minim of Sepphoris and Tiberias in the Second and Third Centuries," *Studies in Jewish History* (1956), pp. 245–74, although his identification of these *minim* is in need of reexamination. See S. Miller, *Studies in the History and Traditions of Sepphoris* (1984), pp. 7f.

31. Neusner, *Eliezer* I, p. 401.

32. Cf. *Qohelet Rabbah* to Eccl. 1:8 (parashah 1:4) and Herford, pp. 215–18, for a much later reflection of the same lesson.

33. B. 'Avodah Zarah 16b–17a; *Qohelet Rabbah* to Eccl. 1:8. Note also the Aramaic narrative in amoraic context (probably Babylonian) in B. Shabbat 116a–b (cf. uncensored texts and Herford, pp. 146–55). This story has Imma Shalom, the wife of Rabbi Eliezer ben Hyrcanus, and her brother Rabban Gamliel II, shortly after the destruction of the Temple, mocking a Jewish Christian judge in their

neighborhood, most probably near Yavneh. Since we cannot substantiate an early date or Palestinian provenance for this story, it has been omitted from this study.

VII.   Conclusion: The Final Break

1. According to some views, the emperor Nerva (ruled 97–98 C.E.) exempted the Christians from the *fiscus judaicus*, thereby declaring Christianity a separate religion (cf. Bruce, p. 390).

2. While the view that Rabbi Akiva declared Bar Kokhba to be the Messiah has been rightly challenged (P. Schäfer, "Rabbi Aqiva and Bar Kokhba," *Approaches to Ancient Judaism* II, ed. W. S. Green [1980], pp. 113–30, also appeared in expanded form in German in his *Studien*, pp. 65–121), the Messianic overtones of his revolt are certainly evidenced by the coinage. See Schürer I (1973), pp. 544f.

3. See Rhoads, pp. 50, 100, 114, 117, 142–4, 146, 148, 172f., 180.

4. Moore, "Jewish Canon," pp. 123f.

5. Justin Martyr and Eusebius in Schürer I (1973), p. 545 n. 141.

6. Schürer I (1973), pp. 553–5.

7. See Schürer I (1973), pp. 536–40, 555.

8. Bruce, pp. 390–2; B. J. Kidd, *A History of the Church* (1922) I, pp. 85–90.

9. For the Rabbinic attitude to Christians after Bar Kokhba, see Urbach, *Ḥazal*, p. 485.

10. For a summary, see Klijn and Reinink, pp. 3–73.

11. Klijn and Reinink, pp. 135 (Origen, referring to the Ebionites), 173 (Epiphanius, referring to the Nazoraeans), 249 (Theodoret of Cyr, referring to the Nazoraeans).

12. Klijn and Reinink, pp. 129 (Origen, referring to the Ebionites), 151 (Eusebius, referring to the Ebionites), 205 (Jerome, calling Ebion a "half-Christian and half-Jew."), 273 (Honorius Augustodunensis, calling Ebionites "half-Jews"). It is apparent that Isidorus and Honorius are dependent on Jerome.

13. Klijn and Reinink, p. 173 (cf. pp. 44f.).

14. The Ebionites did not accept the sanctity and canonicity of the entire Hebrew Bible. See Schoeps, pp. 94–98.

Glossary

ABBA SAUL. Mid-second-century tanna, probably a student of Rabbi Akiva's, sage of the Yavnean period.

'AGGADAH. The class of rabbinic literature which explains the Bible homiletically, as opposed to the *halakhah,* or legal traditions. A general term for stories and traditions regarding biblical heroes and great rabbis, parables, wise sayings, and homilies which have been recorded in the Talmud and the Midrashim.

AGRIPPA I. Tetrarch of Batanea and the Galilee (37–41 C.E.) and king of Judea (41–44 C.E.), grandson of Herod. While king of Judea, his policies were generally pro-Jewish and pro-Pharisaic.

AGRIPPA II. Great-grandson of Herod; last king of the Herodian line, 28–92 C.E.. Although he was never king of Judea, he was appointed by Claudius to supervise the Jerusalem Temple. He was generally sympathetic to Jewish religious practices.

AKIVA, RABBI. Foremost sage of the Yavnean period, c. 50–135 C.E. He had a monumental impact on the development of the *halakhah* in his time, and was martyred by the Romans during the Bar Kokhba Rebellion.

AMORA(IM). Scholars who were active from the completion of the Mishnah (c. 200 C.E.) until the completion of the Gemara (end of fifth century). Their statements constitute the main part of the Talmuds.

'APIQOROS. One who denies God's involvement in the affairs of men and the world.

APOSTATE. One whose actions are not consonant with the standards of behavior set by his religious community.

BARAITA'. An Aramaic term for a statement of law, historical or aggadic tradition which is attributed to the tannaitic period but which is not contained in the Mishnah.

BAR KOKHBA REVOLT. Revolt of Jews against the Romans, 132–135
C.E. Because of the Messianic aspects of this revolt, it did much
to separate the Jewish community from that of the early Christians.

BIRKAT HA-MINIM. A benediction inserted in the Eighteen Benedictions which asks God to obliterate the *minim*. *See* MINIM.

CAIRO GENIZAH. Storehouse or archive of the Jewish community of
Egypt between the ninth and thirteenth centuries. It was discovered in the late nineteenth century and yielded many important Hebrew manuscripts.

DEAD SEA SECT. A Jewish eschatological group which flourished
between 134 B.C.E. and 68 C.E. at the shores of the Dead Sea. The
Dead Sea Scrolls were found in the caves nearby and apparently
constituted their library. This corpus includes both biblical
books and sectarian compositions.

ELEAZAR BEN DAMAH, RABBI. Early-second-century C.E. tanna. He
was the nephew of Rabbi Ishmael. He apparently had some
interest in the study of Greek culture.

ELEAZAR BEN ZADOK, RABBI. The first tanna by this name lived during
the Temple period, in the end of the first and beginning of the
second century C.E. Traditions attributed to him preserve
information about the Temple and its rituals in the last years
before the destruction.

ELIEZER BEN HYRCANUS, RABBI. Sage of the period between the Great
Revolt and the Bar Kokhba rebellion (late first or early second
century C.E.). He was among the most important sages of Yavneh
and was a teacher of Rabbi Akiva.

ELIEZER BEN JACOB, RABBI. The earlier tanna by this name lived
through the destruction of the Second Temple. Teachings attributed to him describe the construction and the furnishings of
the Temple. The later tanna lived in the second century and was
a pupil of Rabbi Akiva.

EPIPHANIUS. Christian author, c. 315–403 C.E. He was born in Palestine and later resided in Thebes, where he established a monas-
tery, and in Cyprus, where he was bishop.

ESSENES. An ascetic sect described by Josephus which flourished from the Hasmonean period (c. 134 B.C.E.) until the destruction in 66–74 C.E. The Essenes are often identified with the sectarians at Qumran (Dead Sea Sect).

'EVED KENA'ANI. Literally "The Canaanite slave," a non-Jewish servant who was circumcised and who, upon manumission, was considered a convert to Judaism.

GAMLIEL II, RABBAN. Patriarch at Yavneh from c. 80 C.E., grandson of the Gamaliel of the New Testament. He probably died before c. 116 C.E. He concentrated his efforts on the unification of the people around Torah after the destruction of the Temple.

GEMARA. The traditions of the amoraim which constituted an analysis and explanation of the Mishnah. Gemara' came to be a synonym for Talmud. There are two distinct Gemarot, the Palestinian and the Babylonian.

GOD-FEARER. *See* SEMI-PROSELYTE.

GREAT REVOLT. Rebellion of Jews against the Romans, 66–74 C.E. This revolt led to the devastation of the country and the destruction of the Jerusalem Temple.

HADRIAN, PUBLIUS AELIUS. Roman emperor (117–138 C.E.) who crushed the Bar Kokhba Revolt and instituted laws making it a capital offense to practice Judaism.

HALAKHAH. The Jewish legal system, and, ultimately, the basis of all aspects of Judaism; the Jewish way of life. *Halakhah, halakhot* —specific law(s).

HALAKHIC MIDRASH. Midrashim edited in Palestine during the amoraic period which contain material attributed to the tannaim. As distinct from the later Midrashim, these texts contain large amounts of halakhic material.

HASMONEANS. The priestly family of the Maccabees and a designation for the dynasty they established. They successfully opposed the Hellenistic reform and the subsequent Seleucid oppression by Antiochus and reconquered the Temple in 164 B.C.E. In 63 B.C.E. the Hasmonean kingdom was conquered by Rome.

HELENA AND IZATES OF ADIABENE. Proselytes, c. 30 C.E. They were members of the royal family of a small kingdom in the upper Tigris region, and their conversion was a source of great pride to Josephus.

HELLENISM. The amalgamation of Greek culture with the native Near Eastern cultures. While this process had begun even beforehand, it was greatly accelerated with the coming of Alexander to the Near East in 334 B.C.E.

HERETIC. One whose beliefs do not accord with those of the established religion to which he claims adherence.

HEROD. Roman client king of Judea from 37 B.C.E. until 4 B.C.E. While distinguished for his great building projects, including the remodeling of the Jerusalem Temple and the port of Caesarea, his questionable status as a Jew and his dissolute life led to widespread opposition to his rule.

HOUSE OF HILLEL, HOUSE OF SHAMMAI. Two groups of sages founded by the great teachers of the late Second Temple period, Hillel and Shammai, who lived at the end of the first century B.C.E. and the beginning of the first century C.E. These two schools were active until the beginning of the second century C.E. Tannaitic literature records numerous debates between the two schools on matters of *halakhah*.

IDUMEANS. People inhabiting the region south of Judea who were conquered by John Hyrcanus (ruled 134–104 B.C.E.), a Hasmonean ruler, and forcibly converted to Judaism.

ISHMAEL, RABBI. Tanna of the first half of the second century C.E. whose teachings were formative to the development of Rabbinic Judaism. (According to our sources, he often argued with Rabbi Akiva.)

JEROME. Christian author, 342–420 C.E. Jerome studied in Syria, where he learned Hebrew. He traveled extensively in Palestine and eventually settled in Bethlehem. There he translated the Bible from the original Hebrew into Latin. He was in contact with various Jewish teachers.

JOHN HYRCANUS. High priest and ethnarch of Judea (135–104 B.C.E.). Always at war, he was able in 129 to consolidate an independent kingdom in Judea.

JOSEPHUS (FLAVIUS). Jewish historian (c. 38–c. 100 C.E.) of the war against Rome whose writings preserve many details of the Second Temple period unknown from any other source.

JOSHUA BEN HANANIAH, RABBI. Sage of the period between the Great Revolt and the Bar Kokhba Revolt (late first or early second century C.E.).

JUDAH THE PRINCE, RABBI. Final redactor of the Mishnah and patriarch of Judea (latter part of the second century and beginning of the third century C.E.). During his office, the patriarchate reached its greatest influence with the Roman government. Due to his importance, he is known simply as "Rabbi" in tannaitic literature.

JUSTIN MARTYR. Christian philosopher and apologist (c. 100–165 C.E.). After accepting Christianity at age 30, he traveled and engaged in disputations with pagan philosophers. He was beheaded by the Romans for refusing to offer a sacrifice to the gods.

KIPPURIM. "Atonement." The phrase "lacking in atonement" is a technical term for one who has completed the necessary purification rituals but may not yet eat the sacrifices of the Temple until he brings an offering.

MACCABEAN REVOLT. The revolt of the Jews against Hellenism in the years 168–164 B.C.E. Although the Hellenistic reform was originated by pro-Hellenistic Jews, the anti-Hellenists soon found themselves fighting as well against the Seleucid Empire. The Jewish victory is celebrated in the holiday of Hanukkah.

MAMZER, MAMZERIM. The Jewish offspring of a forbidden marriage whose ancestry disqualified him from marriage with free, hereditary Jews of the classes priest, Levite, or Israelite.

MESHUMMAD. Literally, "one who has been destroyed," one who forsakes his religion and ignores its regulations. The *meshummad le-hakh'is* is rebelling against religious dicta; the *meshummad le-te'avon* has strayed due to his desire to experience that which is forbidden according to religious law.

MIDRASH HALAKHAH. Tannaitic biblical exegesis for the purpose of establishing a matter of Jewish law.

MINIM. Heretics subjected to legal restrictions in an effort to suppress their rejection of Jewish doctrine. In the Rabbinic period, these restrictions were mainly directed against the early Christians.

NABATEANS. The Hellenized Arabs who inhabited Trans-Jordan and the Negev and whose dominion was at its height from 100 B.C.E. to 100 C.E. They spoke Aramaic and controlled important Near Eastern trade routes.

NAZORAEANS. Judaizing Christian sect (not to be confused with Nazarenes, a general term for Christians).

NOACHIDE LAWS. Commandments which, according to Rabbinic law, are incumbent upon non-Jews.

ORAL LAW. A second Torah which, together with the written Torah, was believed to have been given to Moses at Sinai. This oral Torah contains, according to the Rabbis, the authoritative interpretation of the written Law.

ORIGEN. Church father and theologian (c. 185 C.E.–c. 254 C.E.) who studied Hebrew and used his knowledge to prepare an edition of the Hebrew Bible, the Septuagint, and other Greek translations.

PASCHAL SACRIFICE. Offering made in the Temple on the fourteenth of Nisan, the eve of Passover.

PHARISEES. A sect of Jews in the Second Commonwealth who, according to Talmudic tradition, were the forerunners of the Mishnaic Rabbis (tannaim). The name, literally "separated," indicates their separation from those who did not observe the laws of Levitical tithing and the eating of ordinary meals in ritual purity.

PHILO. Alexandrian Jewish philosopher and Jewish communal leader (c. 20 B.C.E.–50 C.E.). Among his works are extensive discussions of many aspects of Jewish law.

SADDUCEES. A sect known to have existed from the Hasmonean period (134 B.C.E.) to the destruction of the Temple (70 C.E.). This group was led by aristocratic and priestly families and was often in disagreement with the Pharisaic approach to Jewish law and theology.

SAMARITANS. Descendants of those North Israelites who remained in the land after the conquest of the North in 722 B.C.E. and those foreigners brought in by the Assyrians to assure the subservience of the population. After establishing their temple on Mount Gerizim, the Samaritans were in constant conflict with the Jews throughout the Hasmonean and Roman periods.

SELEUCIDS. The ruling dynasty of Syria from the breakup of the empire of Alexander the Great until the Roman conquest. Their support for the extreme Hellenizers brought them into conflict with the Jews in the Maccabean Revolt.

SEMI-PROSELYTE. A non-Jew in the Greco-Roman period who adopted the customs and practices of Judaism without converting according to Jewish law.

SEPPHORIS. A Jewish city located in the Galilee. In the time of Rabbi Judah the Prince, it was the seat of the Patriarchate and the *Bet Din*.

SHA'AṬNEZ. The combination of wool and linen woven together in a garment, forbidden by the Torah.

SIMEON BEN ELEAZAR, RABBI. Second-century tanna, contemporary of Rabbi Judah the Prince. Many of his *halakhot* are cited in *baraitot*.

RABBI SIMEON BEN YOḤAI. Second-century C.E. tanna who was one of the few students of Rabbi Akiva to survive the Bar Kokhba Revolt. As the teacher of Rabbi Judah the Prince, many of his teachings were incorporated into the Mishnah. During the Hadrianic persecutions he was sentenced to death by the Romans and was forced to go into hiding.

TANNA(IM). The Pharisaic-Rabbinic teachers of the period between the Roman conquest of 63 B.C.E. and the editing of the Mishnah by Rabbi Judah the Prince, c. 200 C.E. It was through their efforts that the basis was laid for Talmudic Judaism.

ṬARFON, RABBI. Tanna of the second generation of tannaim, he was a young man at the time of the destruction of the Temple. Later he became a sage of Yavneh, where many of his recorded halakhic discussions were held with Rabbi Akiva.

TETRAGRAMMATON. The four-letter divine name considered by the

Jews to represent the most holy of all names of God. The pronunciation of this name was kept a well-guarded secret in Rabbinic times. It was forbidden to erase this name or to otherwise discard texts in which it had been written.

USHA. The city at which scholars surviving the Bar Kokhba Revolt convened in about the year 140 C.E. There they reconstituted the office of Patriarch, reinstituted the study of Torah, and began to enact *halakhah* once again. This period was particularly important for the compilation of the Mishnah.

YAVNEH. A Jewish city from the time of the Hasmoneans to the Bar Kokhba Revolt, it was the center for scholars and Rabbis between 70 and 132 C.E. under Rabbi Yoḥanan ben Zakkai and Rabban Gamliel II. The *Bet Din* of Yavneh replaced the Jerusalem Sanhedrin after the destruction of the Temple. It was at Yavneh that Judaism was adapted to the post-destruction era.

YOḤANAN BEN ZAKKAI, RABBI. Tanna of the first century C.E., he was the leading Rabbinic personality in the years before the destruction of the Second Temple and shortly thereafter. While the Temple stood, he was involved in controversies with the Sadducees. After the destruction, he worked to establish the center of Rabbinic learning at Yavneh.

YOSE BEN JUDAH, RABBI. Tanna of the second century C.E., contemporary of Rabbi Judah the Prince, with whom he often argues. Statements attributed to him appear often in the Mishnah and Tosefta.

YOSE HA-GELILI, RABBI. Tanna at Yavneh of the second century C.E. who conducted many discussions with Rabbis Akiva and Ṭarfon.

Bibliography

Abrahams, I., *Studies in Pharisaism and the Gospels,* 1st ser., Cambridge: 1917. Reprint. New York: Ktav, 1967.

Albeck, Ch., *Meḥqarim Bi-Baraita' We-Tosefta', We-Yaḥasan La-Talmud,* Jerusalem: Mosad Harav Kook, 1969.

——, ed., *Shishah Sidre Mishnah,* 6 vols., Jerusalem and Tel Aviv: Mosad Bialik and Dvir, 1957–59.

Alon, G., *Jews, Judaism, and the Classical World,* Jerusalem: Magnes Press, 1977.

——, *Meḥqarim Be-Toledot Yisra'el,* 2 vols., Israel: Hakkibutz Hameuchad, 1967, 1970.

——, *Toledot Ha-Yehudim Be-'Ereṣ Yisra'el Bi-Tequfat Ha-Mishnah We-Ha-Talmud.,* 2 vols., Tel Aviv: Hakkibutz Hameuchad, 1967.

Aptowitzer, V., *"Spuren des Matriarchats im jüdischen Schrifttum (Schluss und Nachträge),"* *HUCA* 5 (1928), pp. 261–97.

Babylonian Talmud, Codex Munich, 3 vols., Jerusalem: Sefer, 1971.

Babylonian Talmud, 12 vols., Venice: D. Bomberg, 1520–23.

Babylonian Talmud, ed. Vilna, with commentaries and Alfasi, 20 vols., New York: Otzar Hasefarim, 1964.

Babylonian Talmud, Codex Florence (Florence National Library II i 7–9), 3 vols., Jerusalem: Makor, 1972.

Babylonian Talmud, Manuscripts from the Collection of the Vatican Library, 6 vols., Jerusalem: Makor, 1972–74.

Babylonian Talmud, Tractate 'Abodah Zarah, ed. S. Abramson, New York: Jewish Theological Seminary, 1957.

Babylonian Talmud, Tractate Ḥullin, Codex Hamburg 169, Jerusalem: Makor, 1972.

Bacher, W., *"Der Ausdruck* מוּמָר *in den Handschriften des Talmuds,"* *ZHB* 12 (1908), pp. 39f.

——, *'Erkhe Midrash,* trans. A. Rabinowitz, 2 vols., Tel Aviv: 1922/3.

Bamberger, B., *Proselytism in the Talmudic Period*, New York: Ktav, 1968.

Baron, S. W., *A Social and Religious History of the Jews*, 2nd ed., 16 vols., New York, London, and Philadelphia: Columbia University Press and Jewish Publication Society, 1952–.

Belkin, S., *Philo and the Oral Law*, Cambridge, Mass.: Harvard University Press, 1940.

Ben-Yehudah, E., *Millon Ha-Lashon Ha-'Ivrit*, 8 vols., New York and London: Thomas Yoseloff, 1959.

Bereshit Rabba', ed. J. Theodor and Ch. Albeck, 3 vols., Jerusalem: Wahrmann, 1965.

Blidstein, G., "Who is Not a Jew?—The Medieval Discussion," *ILR* 11 (1976), pp. 369–90.

Bonfil, D., *Ḥiddushe Rabbenu David Bonfil*, vol. 1, ed. Y. Lipshitz, in *Sanhedre Gedolah*, Jerusalem: Harry Fischel Institute, 1966/7.

Brown, F., S. Driver, and C. Briggs, *A Hebrew and English Lexicon of the Old Testament*, Oxford: University Press, 1966.

Bruce, F. F., *New Testament History*, Garden City, N.Y.: Doubleday, 1972.

Büchler, A., "The Levitical Impurity of the Gentile in Palestine before the Year 70," *JQR* n.s. 17 (1926/7), pp. 1–81.

———, "The Minim of Sepphoris and Tiberias in the Second and Third Centuries," *Studies in Jewish History*, London, New York, and Toronto: Oxford University Press, 1956.

Coggins, R. J., *Samaritans and Jews*, Atlanta: John Knox Press, 1975.

Daube, D., "Conversion to Judaism and Early Christianity," *Ancient Jewish Law, Three Inaugural Lectures*, Leiden: E. J. Brill, 1981.

Deutsch, G., "Apikoros," *JE* 1, pp. 665f.

Dexinger, F., "Limits of Tolerance in Judaism: The Samaritan Example," *Jewish and Christian Self-Definition*, vol. 2, ed. E. P. Sanders, Philadelphia: Fortress Press, 1981, pp. 88–114, 327–38.

Elbogen, I., *Ha-Tefillah be-Yisra'el*, Tel Aviv: Dvir, 1972.

Encyclopaedia Judaica, 16 vols., Jerusalem: Keter, 1971/2.

'Enṣiqlopedyah Miqra'it, 5 vols., Jerusalem: Mosad Bialik, 1965–82.

'*Enṣiqlopedyah Talmudit*, 16 vols., Jerusalem: Talmudic Encyclopedia, 1951–.

Epstein, J. N., *Mavo' Le-Nusah Ha-Mishnah*, 2 vols., Jerusalem and Tel Aviv: Magnes Press and Dvir, 1963/4.

———, *Mevo'ot Le-Sifrut Ha-'Amora'im*, Jerusalem and Tel Aviv: Magnes Press and Dvir, 1962.

———, *Mevo'ot Le-Sifrut Ha-Tanna'im*, Jerusalem and Tel Aviv: Magnes Press and Dvir, 1957.

Eusebius, *Historiae Ecclesiasticae*, ed. F. A. Heinichen, 3 vols., Leipzig: Kayser et Schumann, 1827–28.

Finkel, A., "Yavneh's Liturgy and Early Christianity," *Journal of Ecumenical Studies* 18 (1981), pp. 231–46.

Finkelstein, L., "The Institution of Baptism for Proselytes," *JBL* 52 (1933), pp. 203–11.

———, *Mavo' Le-Massekhtot 'Avot We-'Avot De-Rabbi Natan*, New York: Jewish Theological Seminary, 1950.

Flusser, D., "*Ṭevilat Yoḥanan We-Khat Midbar Yehudah,*" *Yahadut U-Meqorot Ha-Naṣerut*, Tel Aviv: Po'alim, 1979, pp. 81–112.

Forkman, G., *The Limits of the Religious Community*, Lund: CWK Gleerup, 1972.

Gilat, Y. D., "Bar Kappara," *EJ* 4, pp. 227f.

———, *Mishnato shel R. 'Eli'ezer ben Hyrcanus*, Tel Aviv: Dvir, 1968.

Ginzberg, L., *Perushim We-Hiddushim Bi-Yerushalmi*, 4 vols., New York: Jewish Theological Seminary, 1941–61.

———, *Seride Ha-Yerushalmi*, New York: Jewish Theological Seminary, 1909.

———, *An Unknown Jewish Sect*, New York: Jewish Theological Seminary, 1976.

Halivni, D. Weiss, *Meqorot U-Mesorot, Mo'ed*, Jerusalem: Jewish Theological Seminary, 1974/5.

———, *Meqorot U-Mesorot, Nashim*, Tel Aviv: Dvir, 1968.

———, "*Yesh Mevi'im Bikkurim,*" *Bar-'Ilan* 7–8 (1969/70), pp. 73–79.

Heinemann, I., *Ha-Tefillah Bi-Tequfat Ha-Tanna'im We-Ha-'Amora'im*, Jerusalem: Magnes Press, 1966.

Hekhalot Rabbati. See Jellinek, A. J., and Wertheimer, S.

Herford, R. T., *Christianity in Talmud and Midrash,* London: 1903. Reprint. New York: Ktav, 1975.

Herodotus, [*Historiae*], 4 vols., London and New York: W. Heinemann and G. P. Putnam's Sons, 1920–24.

Heschel, A. J., *Torah min Ha-Shamayim Ba-'Aspaqlaryah shel Ha-Dorot,* 2 vols., London and New York: Soncino, 1965.

Higger, M., ed., *Sheva' Massekhtot Qeṭanot,* Jerusalem: Makor, 1970/1.

The Holy Bible, Oxford Annotated Bible, Revised Standard Version, ed. H. G. May and B. M. Metzger, New York: Oxford University Press, 1962.

Hyman, A., "Maimonides' 'Thirteen Principles,'" *Jewish Medieval and Renaissance Studies,* ed. A. Altmann, Cambridge, Mass.: Harvard University Press, 1967, pp. 119–44.

Hyman, A., *Toledot Tanna'im We-'Amora'im,* 3 vols., Jerusalem: Qiryah Ne'emanah, 1964.

Jastrow, M., *Dictionary of Talmud Bavli, Yerushalmi, Midrashic Literature and Targumim,* 2 vols., New York: Pardes, 1950.

Jellinek, A. J., ed., *Hekhalot Rabbati,* in *Bet Ha-Midrash,* vol. 3, Jerusalem: Wahrmann, 1967, pp. 83–108.

Josephus, [*Works*], trans. H. St. J. Thackeray, R. Marcus, A. Wikgren, and L. Feldman, 9 vols., Cambridge, Mass., and London: Harvard University Press and William Heinemann, 1926–65.

Justini, S., *Cum Tryphone Judaeo Dialogus,* ed. W. Trollope, Cambridge: J. Hall, 1849.

Kanter, S., *Rabban Gamaliel II: The Legal Traditions,* Brown Judaic Studies 8, Chico, Calif.: Scholars Press, 1980.

Katz, J., "'Af 'Al Pi She-Ḥata' Yisra'el Hu'," *Tarbiz* 27 (1957/8), pp. 203–17.

———, *Exclusiveness and Tolerance,* New York: Schocken, 1962.

Kaufmann, Y., *Toledot Ha-'Emunah Ha-Yisra'elit,* 4 vols., Jerusalem and Tel Aviv: Mosad Bialik and Dvir, 1966/7.

Kedar, B., "Netherworld, In the Aggadah," *EJ* 12, pp. 997f.

Kidd, B. J., *A History of the Church,* 3 vols., Oxford: Clarendon Press, 1922.

Kimelman, R., *"Birkat Ha-Minim* and the Lack of Evidence for an Anti-Christian Jewish Prayer," *Jewish and Christian Self-Definition,* vol. 2, ed. E. P. Sanders, Philadelphia: Fortress Press, 1981, pp. 226–44, 391–403.

Kimhi, D., Commentary on Joshua in *Miqra'ot Gedolot,* ed. Venice, 1525. Reprint. Jerusalem: Makor, 1972.

Klijn, A. F. J., and G. J. Reinink, *Patristic Evidence for Jewish-Christian Sects,* Leiden: E. J. Brill, 1973.

Klostermann, E., ed., *Die Griechischen Christlichen Schriftsteller, Origenes III,* Leipzig: J. C. Hinrischs'sche Buchhandlung, 1901.

Kohler, K., "Circumcision," *JE* 4, pp. 91–96.

Kraabel, A. T., "The Disappearance of the 'God-fearers,'" *Numen* 28 (1981), pp. 113–26.

Krauss, S., *Griechische und Lateinische Lehnwörter im Talmud, Midrasch und Targum,* 2 vols., Hildesheim: Georg Olms, 1964.

———, "The Jews in the Works of the Church Fathers," *JQR* o.s. 5 (1893), pp. 122–57.

Lauterbach, J. Z., *Rabbinic Essays,* Cincinnati: Hebrew Union College Press, 1951.

Leiman, S., *The Canonization of Hebrew Scripture,* Hamden, Conn.: The Connecticut Academy of Arts and Sciences, 1976.

Levine, B., "Kippurim," *Eretz Israel* 9 (1969), pp. 88–95.

Lewin, B. M., *'Oṣar Ha-Ge'onim,* 13 vols., Haifa and Jerusalem, 1927/8–1942/3.

Licht, J., *"Milah," 'Enṣiqlopedyah Miqra'it* 4, pp. 894–901.

Liddell, H., and R. Scott, *A Greek-English Lexicon,* revised and augmented by H. Stuart Jones and R. McKenzie, with a supplement, Oxford: University Press, 1968.

Lieberman, S., *Greek in Jewish Palestine,* New York: P. Feldheim, 1965.

———, "How Much Greek in Jewish Palestine?" *Biblical and other Studies,* ed. A. Altmann, Cambridge, Mass.: Harvard University Press, 1963, pp. 123–41. Reprint. *Texts and Studies,* New York: Ktav, 1974, pp. 216–34.

———, Review of Krauss, S., *Tosefot He-'Arukh Ha-Shalem, KS* 14 (1937), pp. 218–228.

———, "Roman Legal Institutions in Early Rabbinics and in the Acta Martyrum, *JQR* n.s. 35 (1944), pp. 1–55. Reprint. *Texts and Studies,* New York: Ktav, 1974, pp. 57–111.

———, "Some Aspects of After Life in Early Rabbinic Literature," *Harry A. Wolfson Jubilee Volume,* Jerusalem: 1965, pp. 495–532. Reprint. in *Texts and Studies,* New York: Ktav, 1974, pp. 235–72.

———, *Tosefet Rishonim,* vols. 1–3, Jerusalem: Bamberger and Wahrmann, 1937–39, vol. 4, Mosad Harav Kook, 1939.

———, *Tosefta' Ki-Fshutah,* 8 vols., New York: Jewish Theological Seminary, 1955–.

Lightstone, J., *Yose the Galilean,* vol. 1, Studies in Judaism in Late Antiquity, vol. 31, Leiden: E. J. Brill, 1979.

Lipschutz, I., *Tiferet Yisra'el,* in *Mishnah,* ed. Vilna, 12 vols. Reprint. New York: Pardes, 1952/3.

Loewenstamm, S., *"Karet, Hikkaret,"* *'Enṣiqlopedyah Miqra'it* 4, pp. 330–2.

———, *"Mamzer,"* *'Enṣiqlopedyah Miqra'it* 5, pp. 1–3.

Lüdemann, G., "The Successors of Pre-70 Jerusalem Christianity: A Critical Evaluation of the Pella-Tradition," *Jewish and Christian Self-Definition,* vol. 1, ed. E. P. Sanders, Philadelphia: Fortress Press, 1980, pp. 161–73, 245–54.

Maḥazor Vitry, ed. S. Hurwitz, Jerusalem: Alef Publishing, 1963.

Maier, J., *Jesus von Nazareth in der talmüdischen Überlieferung,* Darmstadt, 1978.

Maimonides, M., *Mishneh Torah,* ed. Vilna, 5 vols., reprinted with additions, Jerusalem: Pardes, 1955.

———, *Perush Ha-Mishnayot,* in *Babylonian Talmud,* ed. Vilna.

———, *Perush Ha-Mishnayot,* in *Mishnah,* ed. Naples, 1492.

Mann, J., "Genizah Fragments of the Palestinian Order of Service," *HUCA* 2 (1925), pp. 269–338.

Marmorstein, A., "The Amidah of the Public Fast Days," *JQR* n.s. 15 (1924), pp. 415–17.

———, "Judaism and Christianity in the Middle of the Third Century," *HUCA* 10 (1935), pp. 223–63.

Meeks, W. A., "'Am I a Jew?' — Johanine Christianity and Judaism," *Christianity, Judaism and other Greco-Roman Cults, Studies for Morton Smith at Sixty,* ed. J. Neusner, part 1, Leiden: E. J. Brill, 1975, pp. 163–86.

Mekhilta' De-Rabbi Ishma'el, ed. H. S. Horovitz, and I. A. Rabin, Jerusalem: Bamberger and Wahrmann, 1960.

Mekhilta' De-Rabbi Shim'on ben Yoḥai, ed. D. Hoffmann, Frankfurt am Main: J. Kaufmann, 1905.

Midrash 'Aggadah, ed. S. Buber, Vienna: A. Panto, 1893/4.

Midrash Tanḥuma', ed. S. Buber, New York: Sefer, 1946.

Midrash Tanna'im, ed. D. Hoffmann, Berlin: Itzkowski, 1909.

Miller, S., "Proselytes and God-fearers in Non-Rabbinic Sources of the First Century C.E.," unpublished seminar paper, 1975.

——, *Studies in the History and Traditions of Sepphoris,* Leiden: E. J. Brill, 1984.

Mishna, Sedarim Zeraim, Moed, Nashim, Unknown Edition Pisaro or Constantinople, Jerusalem: Makor, 1970.

Mishnah, Codex Kaufmann, 2 vols., Jerusalem: Sifriyat Meqorot, 1967/8.

Mishnah, Codex Paris 328–9, Introduction by M. Bar-Asher, 3 vols., Jerusalem: Makor, 1973.

Mishnah, Codex Parma, De Rossi 138, 2 vols., Jerusalem: Kedem, 1970.

Mishnah, Codex Parma "C," De Rossi 984, Sedarim Nashim, Neziqin, Jerusalem: Makor, 1971.

Mishnah, ed. Ch. Albeck, with vocalization by H. Yalon, 6 vols., Jerusalem and Tel Aviv: Mosad Bialik and Dvir, 1957–59.

Mishnah, ed. W. H. Lowe (*The Mishnah on which the Palestinian Talmud Rests*), 2 vols., Cambridge: University Press, 1883.

Mishnah, ed. Vilna, 12 vols., New York: Pardes, 1952/3.

Mishnah 'im Perush Ha-Rambam, ed. princ., Naples, 1492, Introduction by A. M. Habermann, 2 vols., Jerusalem: Sifriyat Meqorot, 1969/70.

Moore, G. F., "The Definition of the Jewish Canon and the Repudiation of Christian Scriptures," *The Canon and Masorah of the Hebrew Bible: An Introductory Reader,* ed. S. Leiman, New York: Ktav, 1974, pp. 115–41.

Neusner, J., *Eliezer ben Hyrcanus, the Tradition and the Man,* 2 parts, Leiden: E. J. Brill, 1973.

———, *A History of the Mishnaic Law of Holy Things,* 6 parts, Leiden: E. J. Brill, 1978–80.

———, *A History of the Mishnaic Law of Purities,* 22 parts, Leiden: E. J. Brill, 1974–77.

———, *A History of the Mishnaic Law of Women,* 5 parts, Leiden: E. J. Brill, 1980.

———, "Rabbinic Traditions about the Pharisees before A.D. 70: The Problem of Oral Tradition," *JJS* 22 (1971), pp. 1–18.

Nissim ben Reuven Gerondi (pseudo-), *Ḥiddushe Ha-Ran 'al Massekhet Sanhedrin,* in *Babylonian Talmud,* ed. Vilna.

Origen, *Selectorum in Psalmos,* in *Origenis, Opera Omnia,* ed. C. H. E. Lommatzsch, 3 parts, vols. 11, 12, 13, Berolini: Sumtibus Hande et Spencer, 1841.

Palestinian Talmud, ed. Krotoschin. Reprint. Jerusalem: Torah La-'Am, 1959/60.

Palestinian Talmud, ed. Venice: D. Bomberg, 1523/24.

Palestinian Talmud, ed. Vilna, 7 vols. Reprint. New York: Otzar Hasefarim, 1958/9.

Palestinian Talmud, ed. Zhitomir. Reprint. Jerusalem: Bene Ma'arav, 1979/80.

Palestinian Talmud, Manuscript Leiden, 4 vols. Reprint. Jerusalem: Makor, 1970/1.

Pardo, D., *Ḥasde David,* 5 vols., I, Leghorn: 1776; II, Leghorn: 1789/90; III, Jerusalem: 1889/90; IV, Jerusalem: 1970; V, Jerusalem: 1971.

Passamaneck, S. M., "Some Medieval Problems in *Mamzeruth,*" HUCA 37 (1966), pp. 121–45.

Porges, [N.], *"Der Ausdruck* מוּמָר *in den Handschriften des Talmuds,"* ZHB 12 (1908), pp. 108–10.

———, "*Der Talmud Jeruschalmi zu Chullin und Bechoroth,*" ZHB 11 (1907), p. 158.

Porton, G., *The Traditions of Rabbi Ishmael,* 4 parts, Leiden: E. J. Brill, 1976–80.

Preuss, J., *Biblical and Talmudic Medicine,* trans. and ed. F. Rosner, New York, London: Sanhedrin Press, 1978.

Qohelet Rabbah, in *Midrash Rabbah,* ed. Vilna, 2 vols., New York: Grossman, 1952.

Rabbinovicz, R. N., *Diqduqe Soferim,* 15 vols., New York, Jerusalem and Montreal: 1959/60.

Rabin, C., *Qumran Studies,* Oxford: University Press, 1957.

Ran. See Nissim ben Reuven Gerondi.

Rhoads, D., *Israel in Revolution, 6–74 C.E.,* Philadelphia: Fortress Press, 1976.

Rist, J. M., *Epicurus,* Cambridge: University Press, 1972.

Rokeah, D., "*Ben Ṣṭara', Ben Panṭira' Hu',*" *Tarbiz* 39 (1969/70), pp. 11–15.

Rowley, H. H., "Jewish Proselyte Baptism and the Baptism of John," *HUCA* 15 (1940), pp. 313–34. Reprint. *From Moses to Qumran,* London and New York: Association Press, 1963, pp. 211–35.

Sanders, E. P., *Paul and Palestinian Judaism,* Philadelphia: Fortress Press, 1977.

Schäfer, P., "Rabbi Akiva and Bar Kokhba," *Approaches to Ancient Judaism,* vol. 2, ed. W. S. Green, Chico, Calif.: Scholars Press, 1980.

———, *Studien zur Geschichte und Theologie des Rabbinischen Judentums,* Leiden: E. J. Brill, 1978.

Schalit, A., *Yosef ben Matityahu (Flavius Yosefus), Qadmoniyyot Ha-Yehudim,* vol. 3, Jerusalem: Mosad Bialik, 1973.

Schechter, S., "Genizah Specimens," *JQR* o.s. 10 (1898), pp. 654–9.

Schiffman, L. H., "*Giyyur Be-Khitve Yosef ben Matityahu, Izates Me-Hadayev Le-'Or Ha-Halakhah,*" *Yosef ben Matityahu, Historion shel 'Ereṣ Yisra'el,* ed. U. Rappaport, Jerusalem: Yad Ishaq ben Zvi, 1982.

————, *The Halakhah at Qumran,* 2 vols., Brandeis University Doctoral Dissertation, Waltham, Mass.: 1974.

————, "Jewish Sectarianism in Second Temple Times," *Great Schisms in Jewish History,* ed. R. Jospe, S. Wagner, New York: Center for Judaic Studies and Ktav, 1981, pp. 1–46.

————, *Sectarian Law in the Dead Sea Scrolls, Courts, Testimony and the Penal Code,* Brown Judaic Studies 33, Chico, Calif.: Scholars Press, 1983.

Schoeps, H.-J., *Jewish Christianity,* Philadelphia: Fortress Press, 1969.

Scholem, G., *Jewish Gnosticism, Merkabah Mysticism, and Talmudic Tradition,* New York: Jewish Theological Seminary, 1965.

Schürer, E., *A History of the Jewish People in the Age of Jesus Christ,* ed. G. Vermes and F. Millar, 2 vols., Edinburgh: T. and T. Clark, 1973, 1979.

————, *A History of the Jewish People in the Time of Jesus Christ,* trans. S. Taylor and P. Christie, 5 vols., New York: Charles Scribner's Sons, 1891.

Sefer Ha-Razim, ed. M. Margaliot, Jerusalem: American Academy for Jewish Research, 1966/7.

Sifra or Torat Kohanim, according to Codex Assemani LXVI, with Hebrew Introduction by L. Finkelstein, New York: Jewish Theological Seminary, 1956.

Sifra' De-Ve Rav (Torat Kohanim), ed. I. H. Weiss, Vienna: J. Schlossberg, 1861/2.

Sifra' De-Ve Rav (Torat Kohanim), with commentaries, Jerusalem: Sifra, 1958/9.

Sifre De-Ve Rav (Numbers), ed. H. S. Horovitz, Jerusalem: Wahrmann, 1966.

Smallwood, E. M., "The Legislation of Hadrian and Antoninus Pius against Circumcision," *Latomus* 18 (1959), pp. 334–47.

————, "The Legislation of Hadrian and Antoninus Pius against Circumcision: Addendum," *Latomus* 20 (1961), pp. 93–96.

Smith, D. M., "John, Gospel of," *Interpreter's Dictionary of the Bible,* Supplementary Volume, Nashville, Tenn.: Abingdon, 1976, pp. 482–6.

Smith, M., "Early Christianity and Judaism," *Great Confrontations in Jewish History,* ed. S. Wagner and A. Breck, Denver: University of Denver, Department of History, 1977, pp. 39–61.

———, *Jesus the Magician,* London: Victor Gollancz Ltd., 1978.

Sperber, D., "Min." *EJ* 12, pp. 1–3.

———, "Sifrei Ha-Minim," *EJ* 14, p. 1521.

Stern, M., *Greek and Latin Authors on the Jews and Judaism,* 2 vols., Jerusalem: Israel Academy of Sciences and Humanities, 1976.

Strodach, G., *The Philosophy of Epicurus,* Evanston, Ill.: Northwestern University Press, 1963.

Tass, Y., "Ṣara'at," sec. d, *'Enṣiqlopedyah Miqra'it* 4, pp. 776–8.

Tcherikover, V., *Hellenistic Civilization and the Jews,* Philadephia: Jewish Publication Society, 1966.

Tchernowitz, C., *Toledot Ha-Halakhah,* 4 vols., New York: 1945–53.

Tosefot Yeshanim, in *Babylonian Talmud,* ed. Vilna.

Tosefta', ed. S. Lieberman, 4 vols., New York: Jewish Theological Seminary, 1955–.

Tosefta', ed. M. Zuckermandel, Jerusalem: Wahrmann, 1962/63.

Tosefta', in *Hilkhot Rav 'Alfas, editio princeps,* Venice: D. Bomberg, 1521/22.

Tosefta', Manuscript Vienna 46.

Urbach, E. E., *Ḥazal,* Jerusalem: Magnes Press, 1971.

———, "Hilkhot 'Avadim Ke-Maqor Le-Historiyah Ha-Ḥevratit Bi-Yeme Ha-Bayit Ha-Sheni U-Vi-Tequfat Ha-Mishnah We-Ha-Talmud," *Zion* 25 (1960), pp. 141–89.

Weiss, J., *Earliest Christianity,* 2 vols., New York: Harper, 1959.

Wertheimer, S., *Batei Midrashot,* 2 vols., Jerusalem: Ktab Wasepher, 1965/6.

Wolfson, H., *Philo,* Cambridge, Mass.: Harvard University Press, 1968.

Ydit, M., *"Birkat Ha-Minim,"* *EJ* 4, pp. 1035f.

Zeitlin, S., "The Halaka in the Gospels and Its Relation to the Jewish Law in the Time of Jesus," *HUCA* 1 (1924), pp. 357–63.

———, "A Note on Baptism for Proselytes," *JBL* 52 (1933), pp. 78–79.

Index